Gloria Allred Carol Bellamy Linda Bloodworth-Thomason Barbara Boxer Sarah Brady Dixie Carter Nell Carter Cher Hillary Rodham Clinton Jane Curtin Faye Dunaway Sandy Duncan Linda Ellerbee Nora Ephron Jane Fonda Nancy Friday Annette Funicello Phyllis George Ellen Goodman Sue Grafton Marion Hammer Valerie Harper Lauren Hutton Erica Jong Naomi Judd Elaine Kagan Donna Karan Diane Keaton Suzy Kellett Kay Koplovitz Patti LaBelle Ellen Levine Donna Lopiano Susan Love Tammy Faye Bakker Messner Carol Moseley-Braun Anne Murray K. T. Oslin Letty Cottin Pogrebin Stefanie Powers Lynn Redgrave Linda Ronstadt Diane Sawyer Donna Shalala Suzanne Somers Marlo Thomas Nina Totenberg Diane Von Furstenberg Faye

Happy Birthday,
Aunt Donna!!!
Trust me you don't
look 50!!!
Lots of ♥
Julie

Happy
Birthday
Aunt Donna

Love,
Jeff

FIFTY

Wisdom, inspiration, and reflections

ON

on women's lives well lived

BONNIE MILLER RUBIN

FIFTY

WARNER BOOKS
A Time Warner Company

Handwritten inscriptions:

Happy Birthday & Best Wishes Brother Bill

Happy Happy Birthday Donna!

We all love you so much. Sandy

xoxoxo and Jason & Jenni ooo

Warner Books, Inc.
1271 Avenue of the Americas
New York, NY 10020

Visit our Web site at http://www.warnerbooks.com

Ⓦ A Time Warner Company

Printed in Canada

First Printing: November 1998

10 9 8 7 6 5 4 3 2 1

Library of Congress Cataloging-in-Publication Data
Rubin, Bonnie Miller.
        Fifty on fifty : wisdom, inspiration, and reflections on women's lives well lived /
Bonnie Miller Rubin.
            p.   cm.
        Includes fifty black and white portraits.
        ISBN 0-446-52369-0
        1. Middle aged women—United States—Attitudes.   2. Aging—
United States—Psychological aspects.   3. Maturation (Psychology).
4. Success—Case studies.   5. Middle aged women—United States—Biography.
6. Celebrities—United States—Biography.   7. United States—Biography.   I. Title.
II. Title: 50 on 50.
HQ1059.5.U5R83   1998
305.244—DC21   97-18087
                              CIP

Designed by Dania Martinez Davey

ACKNOWLEDGMENTS

All my friends and family have been involved with this project, but a few merit special mention.

My parents—who have always devoured everything I wrote—never tired of scouring newspapers and magazines for possible subjects. Every child—even one approaching her own fiftieth birthday—should know such unconditional love.

Leigh Behrens, my colleague at the *Chicago Tribune*, was always there with an ear and a shoulder when I needed it most. That she is also a smart and thoughtful journalist is merely a bonus.

Susan Lichtenfeld's generous offer of both her time and her talent will never be forgotten. Jane Himmel, too, provided invaluable organization and an eye for detail.

For more than a decade, Jeanne Hanson has been much more than my agent, but an ally and friend whose optimism is as valuable as her business acumen.

This book also belongs to Jackie Merri Meyer, my editor at Warner Books, who believed in the project when others didn't. Her patience and professionalism are deeply appreciated.

To David, my husband and best friend of almost twenty-five years, and my children, Michael and Alyssa, who never complained about all the take-out meals.

And to the women who unabashedly shared their loves and their losses—to say nothing of their birth dates—thank you for showing us the way.

"I thought it was an advantage that I could be different. I didn't have to smoke cigars when everyone else did, or wear red ties when everyone else did. I was an oddity, and it played well."

—GERALDINE LAYBOURNE, broadcast executive

Working Woman magazine

"Who wants to be remembered as merely a gilded mirror, decorative but empty until an influential man shows up?"

— R. Z. SHEPPARD, writer

TIME magazine

Over the course of a year, I had the privilege of conversations with fifty successful and engaging women about their lives, how they had evolved, and more importantly, what they know now that they didn't know when they were younger.

The inspiration hit me while I was trying on bathing suits—in front of a three-way mirror, under fluorescent lights, no less. A dark moment, which neither humor nor prayer can pierce. I was swamped by the feeling that I was not managing the aging process very well.

Yet, when I looked around, others seemed to be doing quite splendidly. At every turn, it seemed, I was treated to yet another account of women composing symphonies, raising valedictorians, amassing fortunes, or achieving inner peace. Every magazine cover featured an obsessively fit-and-lifted actress who knew the secret of making time stand still.

The small knot of fear grew. What if I had just been absent the day everyone got the "aging-well" manual? What if this was something that would elude me forever—like improper fractions?

Right then and there, I decided to pick the collective brains of other women. Perhaps their journeys would help me avoid the potholes and pitfalls of my own. Some are on the cusp of their fiftieth birthday, others are halfway through the decade; still others can see another birthday with a zero looming on the horizon. They come from vastly different backgrounds—it's difficult to imagine two more polar opposites than Tammy Faye Bakker Messner and Donna Shalala—yet, in interview after interview, some universal truths emerged:

• Nothing—not even celebrity—can immunize us from bad times. Each woman had accumulated some dings to the heart—an Alzheimer's parent, a special-needs child, an estranged sibling. There's an old Yiddish saying that, if we all threw our troubles into the middle of the circle, we would want our own back. After fifty interviews, I believe that's true.

• While many women confessed to a full-blown panic attack at turning thirty or forty, there was considerably less anxiety at fifty. Chalk it up to just a few more brushes with the dark side than the last time the odometer turned over. Divorce. Breast cancer. Attending the funeral of at least one peer. If anything, the angst has been replaced by an overwhelming sense of gratitude.

• Conventional wisdom says that our senses are dulled with the passage of time, but if anything, I found women much more attuned to their surroundings—the textures, the flavors, rediscovering what Helen Keller called "my childhood sense of wonderment."

• For all the narcissism associated with baby boomers, the focus has shifted outward. Whether it is Jane Fonda's Georgia Campaign for Adolescent Pregnancy Prevention, Dr. Susan Love's think tank on women's health issues, Faye Wattleton's Center for Gender Equality, or Erica Jong's endowment fund for young writing teachers—the need to nurture others was palpable.

• The clichés about women being competitive with one another—especially as they get older, vying for a diminished pool of available men—were simply not true. Repeatedly, each woman related stories about how the love and loyalty of devoted friends got her over life's icy patches. And with each passing year, they held those friends a little closer, cherished them a little deeper.

• The list of what they wanted out of the next half century became more modest: It boiled down to meaningful work, enduring relationships, good health, and inner contentment.

Maybe that's not so modest after all.

"Someone once described me as a swan. I look so smooth going across the lake, but underneath, I'm paddling like crazy."

—SHELLY LAZARUS, CEO, Ogilvy & Mather

Fortune magazine

FIFTY
ON
FIFTY

"At fifty, I was already a grandmother . . . It is the first time in your life that you will love totally without fear. With your own kids, you worry terribly. If they have trouble with math, somehow you think it's your fault. But with grandchildren, nothing is your fault."

—MARY TRAVERS, folk singer

JULY 3, 1941
ATTORNEY

© Craig Sjodin

Gloria Allred moved from New York to California in the late 1960s—twenty-five years old, a single mother, with two suitcases and about $100 in her pocket. She became one of the nation's most prominent attorneys, associated with every hot-button gender issue of the day: child and domestic abuse, sexual harassment, job discrimination, rape, gay rights. What happened in between wasn't the result of any grand career plan, but rather life itself.

Growing up in Philadelphia, Allred was encouraged by her parents—who only had eighth-grade educations—to set the bar as high as possible. She also found a powerful role model in an aunt who was a heart surgeon ("The only woman I knew who didn't get married, didn't have kids, and didn't cook").

But once out on her own, Allred discoverd life was a cruel teacher.

fifty on fifty

After receiving a master's degree in English from New York University, she taught in the Watts neighborhood of Los Angeles, where she became aware of the inequitable treatment of female teachers. She also had been raped, paid less than a male colleague for doing exactly the same work, and knew what it was like to raise a child alone. An activist was born.

Her growing feminism led to law school (Loyola University), where she felt she could be most effective in "expanding, vindicating, and asserting rights" for women. In 1976, she started her own practice—Allred, Maroko and Goldberg—with two classmates and found a niche handling some of the nation's most topical lawsuits.

In 1988, Allred became the first woman to gain entry in New York's famed Friars Club (which brought a testy exchange with Henny Youngman, who blocked the door). She also took on Saks Fifth Avenue for charging women more for alterations than men.

While these suits have brought notoriety (she has never been accused of being publicity-shy), it is the cases that have broad public impact of which she is most proud. Allred is divorced and lives in Los Angeles.

• • •

When my daughter was little, she said to me one day, "When I grow up, I'm going to be ready with cookies and milk when my daughter comes home from school." Today she is member of our firm—an outstanding attorney and human being—so, all things change.

As women age, they ultimately all learn the same lesson: The only person I can depend on is me.

It's an evolution. It comes out of being a single parent, sexual harassment at work, being paid less than a man, needing an abor-

"When women are younger, they have little use

tion, suffering domestic abuse, getting a divorce, having problems collecting child support . . . these are life experiences for most women. They're also the kinds of radicalizing experiences that caused me to be a feminist.

My commitment grew because I came personally to understand the extent and scope of the problem. For example, one woman who wanted to be a police officer was asked during the interview process whether or not she used contraceptives or had ever had an abortion. There were many cases like that, which we won. Only after I entered my law practice did I realize the widespread pattern of discrimination. And that's when I knew it was my duty to change it.

When women are younger, they have little use for feminism. They don't recognize the need. They have stars in their eyes and think Prince Charming will still come along. But older women are more realistic. They become more radical as they get older. Divorce is radicalizing . . . so is being on the job and health issues—the fact that more money is spent on medical research for men than women. They become more radical because they've been burned more often. In many ways, younger women are going to be more shocked, more disappointed than my generation because our expectations were lower.

I am not ashamed to tell people how old I am or that I'm a grandmother. I wouldn't go back to being nineteen for anything. Women should get a medal just for surviving. With each passing year, I become a more committed feminist. The only reason I got into law school was because of the other women who came before me.

So my advice is that each one of us has a duty to help improve the status of women. The one thing I know is that we cannot let these wrongs go unaddressed. We need to make it a better world for our daughters, so they don't have to suffer the way we have suffered.

for feminism. They don't recognize the need . . . But older women are more realistic."

CAROL BELLAMY

JANUARY 14, 1942
EXECUTIVE DIRECTOR, UNICEF

© Unicef

4

Anyone who likes to chart career paths would be intrigued by Carol Bellamy's zigs and zags.

She started out as a Peace Corps volunteer, serving in a remote village in Guatemala and eager to change the world. For that, she would need a law degree, but when she graduated from New York University School of Law in 1968, she didn't open the urban storefront practice, as expected. Instead, she headed for a tony Manhattan law firm, followed by Wall Street, where she rose in the cutthroat world of investment banking.

After being steeped in such raw capitalism, she returned to the role of public servant, including a stint as New York City Council president—the first woman to ever hold that position. But her political career hit a roadblock when she lost two key campaigns.

She was appointed director of the Peace Corps in 1993, the first former volunteer to ever head the agency. Her Wall Street background has made her a popular choice for an organization in need of sound fiscal management. At her confirmation hearings, Senator Daniel Patrick Moynihan crowed, "We adore you in New York and they're going to love you all over the world."

In 1995, she took over the reins at UNICEF, the United Nations Children's Fund, which had problems of its own, including a corruption scandal at its Nairobi, Kenya, headquarters. It is precisely the kind of organizational turnaround that she thrives on.

Bellamy is single and lives in New York.

"Don't wait too long to do a few other things with your life. Be open to new opportunities."

• • •

I learned my first wisdom early—as a volunteer in the Peace Corps. You never know what's going to happen next, so be prepared.

I've done a lot of different jobs. I would get bored if I had just worked at one place and did the same thing, but there is a difference between risk-taking and gambling: Risk-taking is setting up everything, except there is one unpredictable aspect to what you're doing, so you still have to take that one leap. Gambling is setting up nothing. I'm a risk-taker, not a gambler. After I lost the [New York City mayoral primary] election, a friend reminded me that when doors close, windows open—and that has certainly proven to be true. I do like things anchored, but not tied down.

I don't want to make a habit of failing, but every once in a while, it's not bad to bloody your nose a bit. I've won elections and I've

5

lost elections and I've learned as much if not more by the losses. I probably wouldn't be doing what I'm doing now, which is among the most important work I've ever done. This is about children, which really is about the future. For good or bad, I'd rather be working on tomorrow.

I've loved what has been available to me . . . having half my life in the private sector—as a lawyer and banker—and the other half in the public sector. I've had bad days, but I've never been involved in something that I didn't love. But I'm not sure I'd call it passion. I'm Presbyterian; we don't have much passion.

I grew up in a blue-collar family—my dad was a telephone installer, my mom was a nurse. They went to high school and their parents didn't even do that. And here I am, a lawyer. We didn't have a lot of discussions about choices, but I was encouraged to think broad thoughts.

I'm leery of giving advice—most people have to learn things on their own—but I think it comes down to equal parts of hard work and never forgetting friends and family. I didn't do badly, but I could have spent more time with people . . . and I feel sad about that. My mom died a few years ago and I miss her a lot.

Don't wait too long to do a few other things with your life. Be open to new opportunities. I'm not looking for any new adventures, but I'm not ready to rule anything out, either.

6

LINDA BLOODWORTH-THOMASON

APRIL 15, 1947

TV PRODUCER AND WRITER

courtesy of Linda Bloodworth-Thomason

Linda Bloodworth-Thomason is among a handful of women who have cracked the boys' club of producing and writing for television.

As the co-creator behind Designing Women, Evening Shade, and Hearts Afire, she created characters who refused to be pigeonholed. In each series, she portrayed women—Southern women—who were strong and feminine and didn't live in a trailer park.

Writing has always been a vehicle for what's on her mind and in her heart. When her mother-in-law died of breast cancer, it showed up in an episode of Designing Women. When she lost her own mother to AIDS—contracted through a blood transfusion—it, too, found its way on the air (and an Emmy nomination). To make sure the characters had the ring of authenticity, she wrote *all twenty-two episodes during the show's first season, a rare feat.*

Her earliest ambition was to be the family's first female attorney. Instead, after graduating from the University of Missouri, she headed out to California, where she took a job writing for a Los Angeles law journal, followed by a stint teaching English in the Watts neighborhood of Los Angeles. ("I thought we'd sit around on pillows and read Byron. When I arrived, I found out that I had seventy-seven students and twenty-two chairs and the teacher before me had been raped.")

On a whim, she sent a script to Larry Gelbart, the creative genius behind M*A*S*H. *Gelbart saw a spark, gave her a chance, and she was on her way. She met Harry Thomason, a filmmaker and producer. Married in 1983, they formed Mozark Productions (named for their respective home states of Missouri and Arkansas).*

She is almost as famous for her access to the White House as for her television work. In 1992, she produced the documentary The Man from Hope, *which introduced Bill Clinton at the Democratic National Convention in New York. Despite a flurry of criticism leveled at the first couple for being "too Hollywood," the couple was active in the 1996 campaign, with Harry producing the president's cross-country train trip to the convention and Linda producing the sequel film,* A Place Called America.

To honor her late mother, Claudia, she created The Claudia Company, which provides scholarships for qualified girls in Arkansas and Missouri who would not otherwise attend college.

8

• • •

You never hear a taxi driver saying, "Gee, I'd like to be a brain surgeon," but everyone thinks they can do this business. If they only knew what it

"Perhaps the best you can hope for is that someday the people who walked behind you

takes. Each year, five thousand script ideas come in; of those, fifty will actually be made, ten will get on the air, and one will be a hit.

But I was so young and naive . . . I didn't have a Rolodex, I didn't even have an address book. I thought that if I wrote well, someone would find me. It took me a long time to realize how deals are made and how people all know each other. I was so far from the seat of power, but my naïveté worked to my advantage. I was so unsophisticated about the business that when I was told that the studio "passed" on my first pilot, I thought that was a good thing—you know, like passed in college.

There is a tremendous amount of discrimination in this business and every woman has a story to tell. I happened to arrive at the time when (the industry) was looking for women—when they were considered a novelty—so it was an asset.

As a Southern woman, I was so into that approval. If someone had thrown a rock at me at recess, I had to write a thank-you note. If someone didn't like me, I would have taken a boat to China to straighten it out. I had these two conflicting role models—a mom who was very people-pleasing and a dad who would always say what needed to be said. As for me, I wanted both—I wanted to put on the party dress with my mom and go duck-hunting with my dad.

What I don't understand is women who don't support other women. Whether you like Hillary Clinton or not, you have to admit that she's walked through fire for all of us. I admire people who continue on course regardless. Perhaps the best you can hope for is that someday the people who walked behind you will see the note you left and a lightbulb will go off.

Here's my advice to women: Don't cluster so much; don't spend your time yakking about how unfair things are. Don't be part of the herd.

will see the note you left and a lightbulb will go off."

9

Also, don't whine. My father and sister-in-law died of cancer within six weeks of each other. My brother would sit by his wife's bedside in Texas, then get on a plane and do the same thing with our dad in Missouri. Between Thanksgiving and Christmas in 1986, my mother died of AIDS and my husband's mother died of breast cancer. It was a devastating time . . . but work helped keep me alive. As long as I could write a script, I had a purpose. I also think I'm more compassionate.

And you also get a giant dose of perspective. When all the stories broke about [our friendship with] the Clintons, I thought, "This is nothing." A few yuppie journalists decide to write some snide and silly things about me? Big deal. Compared to what we've been through, this is a walk in the park.

BARBARA BOXER

NOVEMBER 11, 1940
U.S. SENATOR

II

Barbara Boxer has a reputation as a straight shooter in a field of smooth talkers.

She has never shrunk from taking on the system, whether it was exposing the Pentagon for overspending (remember the $7,000 coffeepot?) or leading a march of angry women on the Capitol to delay the Senate's confirmation of Supreme Court nominee Clarence Thomas or demanding public hearings on the sexual harassment charges against Oregon Republican Bob Packwood. That the resolution narrowly lost hardly mattered; she had pushed the issue onto the front page and Packwood resigned rather than face expulsion.

The daughter of a middle-class lawyer from Brooklyn, Boxer had her first brush

© Martin Simon/Saba

with politics in the 1960s, when she organized tenants of her apartment building against a negligent landlord. In 1962, she graduated from Brooklyn College and married her college sweetheart, Stewart. They relocated to the Bay Area, where she raised two children and worked in a variety of jobs—including stockbroker and journalist—before being elected to the Marin County Board of Supervisors.

In 1982, she won a seat in the House, representing California's 6th Congressional District, where she was a favorite of feminists, environmentalists, and others who share her Democratic agenda. She has also earned a reputation as an electrifying speaker. Ten years later, she was elected to the Senate. Boxer has two adult children. Her daughter Nicole is married to Hillary Rodham Clinton's brother Tony.

• • •

Most of us in this age group had very few role models. We didn't really have a road map. It was still very new and exciting. In another ten years, young girls would be very matter-of-fact about their ambitions—they talk about wanting to be a senator or wanting to be president, but when I was a kid, I never dreamed of being in politics.

We became involved because we were moved by a certain issue—like education or the environment. For me, it was the Vietnam War. People thought we were so tough—that we were just like the guys—but actually, we were really innocent. We didn't get in because of backroom deals, but because we cared, we were passionate. When I started, it was about what I wanted for my children; now, it's about what I want for my grandson.

It is easy to get cynical about politics, but what keeps me in it is the fierce belief that the people still want someone who is willing to

"People thought we were so tough—that we were just like the guys—but actually, we were really innocent. We didn't get in because of backroom deals, but because we cared,we were passionate."

go against the grain, who is willing to make the tough calls.

In the 1980s, I remember how I was ridiculed over the $7,000 coffeepot. It was like, "What could you possibly know about the military?" They told me that it was an isolated incident, then the next day I found the hammer, then the wrench. But the way I keep myself grounded is by getting out of the Senate and bringing things to the people. Most folks don't know how much the government should pay for an MX missile, but they know what a hammer should cost.

And with Bob Packwood, I fought for the hearings to be public and there were people who didn't like it and don't like me. When I started, I was so soft and now my skin is so tough.

But that's why it's important that whatever you do, go into it for the right reasons. My ambition was not to be something, but to do something. It has been very hard and very wonderful and I wouldn't trade it for anything.

SARAH BRADY

FEBRUARY 6, 1942
GUN CONTROL ACTIVIST

Her life has been more public than she would have liked. But once her husband, Jim, was shot in an assassination attempt on President Ronald Reagan, there was no other choice: Sarah Brady would take her battle for gun control to the court of public opinion.

14

Now, her name regularly tops "most admired women" lists and she has a seat at the table of power, such as addressing the 1996 Democatic Convention. It has been quite a strange journey for the former schoolteacher and Republican stalwart.

As she earned a reputation for being smart and savvy, Brady started moving up the GOP ladder in the 1970s and was eventually named director of administration for the Republican National Committee. At the same time, her husband was also making some waves of his own, running congressional campaigns in Illinois in the 1960s and serving in the Nixon administration. They married in 1973 and their only child, Scott, was born in 1979.

They rarely mention the event that forever altered their lives. Her official biography, from Handgun Control, Inc.—the Washington-

© Murray Bognovitz

based lobbying group, which she heads—makes no reference to John Hinckley, Jr., or March 30, 1981, the date he aimed his $29 pistol and fired into the presidential entourage as they left a Washington hotel. No hint of what it was like to watch the videotape over and over, while anchors somberly (and incorrectly) reported that Jim Brady was dead.

In 1993, after a decade of work, she watched Bill Clinton sign into law the "Brady Bill," which requires a national waiting period and background check on all handgun purchases through licensed dealers. Her role models are Coretta Scott King and Ethel Kennedy.

. . .

My advice is learn to adjust. We all think what our future will be like and it rarely turns out that way. Life changes for everybody, day in and day out, and the people who don't adjust are the most unhappy of all.

One of the things that bothered me the most [after the shooting] is that we didn't have the same friends. I tell myself that it doesn't have to be a trauma for it to happen—kids get older, people move— so we all have to deal with the same stuff. You just learn to tackle it and move on.

Most of the time, I'm fine, but some days it's the little things— like the dryer breaking down—that cause me to have a breakdown. You know you can't do anything about the big things, so when the little things go wrong, that's where you lose it. I also find it difficult to be around petty people who don't understand how lucky they are to have their health. That type of person annoys me tremendously.

My other advice would be to give yourself permission to feel

15

"We must be willing to change constantly because life demands that of us."

badly, at times. Sometimes I see friends going on trips—which for us is almost an impossibility—and I think, "Why can't we go?" Just because you go through hard times doesn't make you a saint. It is natural to go through a little "Why me?" To feel disappointment, anger, jealousy, to question, to mourn. But where you have to draw the line is at bitterness.

I learned something about naïveté. What I wanted to see [gun control legislation] seemed so logical that I thought it would be a snap. Over the years, the political climate changed and now I feel like the public is with us. They want commonsense solutions, so it's up to us to sell it to the elected officials, who are always the last to catch on. People have asked if I ever considered running for office, but I could never do it. I discovered that I much prefer issue advocacy.

I've also learned that we must be willing to change constantly because life demands that of us.

DIXIE CARTER

MAY 25, 1940
ACTRESS

Dixie Carter cannot remember a time when she didn't want to be an opera star. After graduating from Memphis State University, she took this pent-up ambition and headed to New York City, determined to be a diva. "I thought I'd be the toast of the town," she recalled. "Then came the rude awakening. My voice simply wasn't big enough for opera."

She was adrift until a friend recommended that she audition for Joseph Papp, who was casting a production for Shakespeare in the Park. Despite the fact that she had no acting experience, she landed a role in The Winter's Tale. *She put her career on hold for marriage and the birth of two daughters, but she returned with a vengeance, snaring such plum roles as Anna in Lincoln Center's production of* The King and I *and a regular gig on the daytime soap* The Edge of Night.

fifty on fifty

But in 1986, it was her role as the fiery, outspoken Julia Sugarbaker on Designing Women *that finally brought her the name recognition she had craved for so long. After the series went off the air in 1993, Carter penned her autobiography and did some film work. She lives in Los Angeles with her husband, Hal Holbrook.*

• • •

It sounds corny, but I really and truly believe that it's never too late to go after what you want. As the latest of the late bloomers, I'm proof of that. And when you start your professional ascent at forty, you really appreciate the ride. People ask if I mind if someone bothers me for an autograph when I'm at a restaurant or when I'm shopping . . . and I say, "Are you kidding? This is what I worked so hard for."

My regrets are about my daughters. I should have spent more time with them. They're both Harvard graduates and I'm enormously proud of them, but I'm not sure I always let them know they were more important to me than anything else in the world. I'm not beating myself up over it, I'm just sorry about it and at least I have the good grace to admit it.

I don't believe in growing old gracefully. We send a lot of mixed signals about beauty. We say all that matters is what's on the inside. If that's true, then why do we see Michelle Pfeiffer on magazine covers?

So I decided to get my face done. I didn't go into it lightly . . . my mother, especially, was appalled. She saw it as "messing with the Lord's Creation."

But I made up my mind after seeing the pilot of *Designing Women*—the actress who was nearest my age was ten years younger than me. I thought if this turns out to be my first big success, after

18

all these years of performing, I couldn't bear to be identified as "the older one." So I was chopped and sewn. I had the bottom half done one year, then the top half done the next year. I had no idea how dangerous it could be, but I'd do it again.

The way we sit and stand has an enormous amount to do with how fine we look. I'm absolutely mad for yoga, and good posture is an absolute must, too. Beautiful posture rises straight up from the earth, as if we were planted in it.

"I really and truly believe that it's never too late to go after what you want. As the latest of the late bloomers, I'm proof of that."

I work at bringing beauty into our home, too. I set my table with candles and linens because it matters to me. I believe in ritual and ceremony. But the most important lesson is to bring beauty to your attitude.

Angry youth can be exhilarating, idealistic, and it even makes for good movies. Middle-aged anger, though, is just another kind of failure. It's not good to be around. Whatever it is that is making you negative, get over it; whatever the source, get rid of it. Anger is second-rate and it's really a bit arrogant. It's saying that my troubles are worse than yours.

NELL CARTER

© Dick Wieand

20

The fact that Nell Carter—who would be the first to admit that she doesn't fit the image of a Hollywood starlet—could find success both on the stage and the TV screen is a testimony to her talent. That she could survive both a drug addiction and a double aneurysm is a tribute to her strength.

Ever since making her Broadway debut in 1970 at age twenty-two (in a fluffy piece called Soon, *with Richard Gere), Carter has commanded audiences' attention. Eight years later, she won a Tony Award for her high-voltage performance in the 1978 musical* Ain't Misbehavin'. *The Fats Waller musical was such a hit that it spawned a wave of black cabaret-style reviews, from* Eubie *to* Jelly's Last Jam, *that lasted more than a decade.*

Then, in 1981, Carter was cast in the NBC sitcom Gimme a Break. *The six-year run as sassy housekeeper Nellie Harper brought her two Emmys and, for the first time in her life, "real money."*

But, behind the scenes, life was anything but secure. As one of nine children growing up in Birmingham, Alabama, Carter and her family had a hardscrabble existence. When she was only two years old, she witnessed her father's death, as he accidentally stepped on a live power line. At sixteen, she was raped at gunpoint and had a daughter. By thirty, she struggled with alcohol and cocaine addictions severe enough to require several hospitalizations.

In 1992—at the age of forty-three—her second marriage dissolved, but Carter would face an even more harrowing crisis a few months later. After a bout of severe headaches, she suffered two life-threatening aneurysms. Exactly one year to the day of her surgery and fully recovered, she was cast in ABC's Hangin' with Mr. Cooper.

She lives in New York with her two adopted sons, Joshua and Daniel, both eight years old.

21

• • •

When it comes to marriage, I know that I'm not the type that should be involved in a relationship. Whether I feel bad or wonderful, I'd rather be with a friend who is always truthful with me than to be in a situation that is take, take, take. At this age, I feel that marriage really comprises women doing most of the giving.

The older I am, the more I know that I'm not nearly as wise as I thought I'd be. The difference between having children at an early age and a later age—my kids are twenty years apart—is that the first time, I trained the baby. This time, I learned with the baby. I listen more and preach less. I pay more attention to what the kids have to say. Children will always be honest with you, but we train them to be dishonest. It's so automatic that most people don't even know that they're doing it.

"If you concentrate on doing something to the best of your abilities, you will be rewarded justly."

fifty on fifty

Since the double aneurysms, there's so much more that I know. They knocked me down and made me stop. Now, I find it very easy to say I'm sorry, whereas before, my pride wouldn't let me. I know that fame and fortune can come and go anytime, any way it wants to, but if you concentrate on doing something to the best of your abilities, you will be rewarded justly. And, most of all, never blame others for your failures.

I have no control over whether I get up in the morning. It is a higher power who has given me another day and I try very hard to accept it graciously and thankfully. Everything happens for a reason and I know there was a reason I was given this second chance and second family.

CHER

MAY 20, 1946
SINGER AND ACTRESS

© David Scheinmann

23

Cher's story is as up and down as the Dow Jones average. Rise, fall, rise, fall. Rave reviews, followed by box-office disappointments. The pendulum always swinging between joke (the infomercial queen) and respect (Silkwood, Moonstruck, Mask).

She is fond of quoting music mogul David Geffen's line that she "has more lives than a cat and is using up every one of them."

By her own count, Cher has gone through seven of them during her thirty-four years in show business. It was as singers in the late 1960s that Cher and the late Sonny Bono—husband, and partner— became a sensation. Their nonthreatening hippie act and middle-brow music ("I Got You Babe," "Gypsies, Tramps and Thieves," "Half Breed") played well in a country torn by war and the Watergate scandal.

In 1982—after splitting with Bono—she jumped into films, receiving praise for her role in

"If I make a false move, it's not who I am or what I am. It's just a move."

Come Back to the 5 and Dime, Jimmy Dean, Jimmy Dean. *Her film career peaked five years later with a Best Actress Oscar for* Moonstruck.

Her personal life showed the same gyrations. After Bono, she was linked with Geffen, then married to rock guitarist Gregg Allman, followed by two more long-term relationships with musicians (Gene Simmons of Kiss and Richie Sambora of Bon Jovi). Cher has a twenty-nine-year-old daughter, Chastity Bono, and a son, Elijah Allman, twenty-one. When Chastity came out as a lesbian eight years ago, Cher confessed to having a hard time ("For all my liberal views, I thought I'd react better"), but, today, mother and daughter share a close relationship, she says.

After a five-year hiatus, Cher embarked on yet another comeback in 1996 with a new album, It's a Man's World, *and the film* Faithful— *which lasted in the theaters for about a week before going to video.*

No matter. She retains our affection precisely because her sometimes flawed judgment makes her seem more human than most other pop icons.

. . .

I thought turning fifty was going to be awful . . . but it was a day just like any other day. It's still hard for me to believe, though, because when I think of fifty, I still think of someone like my mom. I mean, I ride a Harley, so I guess that's proof that fifty is going to take on a new form.

I do think that when it comes to aging, we're held to a different standard than men. Some guy said to me, "Don't you think you're too old to sing rock and roll?" I said, "You'd better check with Mick Jagger."

Being sexy has always been a part of my image and I won't shy away from it just because I'm fifty. I'll just continue doing whatever I think is right at the moment. My mother cut all her hair off because she thought after age thirty-five, you shouldn't have long hair. I thought it was strange then and I still think it's strange. You have to do what feels right.

When I was growing up in Southern California, I always thought of myself as unattractive. The role models were like Sandra Dee—cute, perky, blonde. And here I was, dark and moody and strange-looking. It wasn't a nurturing time. School was hard—I think it's not there to teach, but to smooth down the edges so you fit into the round hole. I didn't take to smoothing down those edges very easily.

But my image of myself changed when I started doing something I got some acclaim for. I was the same person I had always been, but the moment you become famous, everything changes. They're looking up at you for exactly the same things that they used to look down on.

It wasn't because of any fear that I had my teeth and nose done. I would have been content to keep them, but I did it for film. Unless I had a certain lighting, my teeth disappeared completely on screen. But otherwise, I'm pretty satisfied.

When you count your life it's full of obviously successful things and some that are not so successful . . . I'm more aware of my failures than anyone else because I have to live with them. If I make a false move, it's not who I am or what I am. It's just a move. I don't spend a lot of time on the failures . . . and I don't spend a lot of time on my successes, either.

"[W]hen you hit [your fifties], being comfortable with yourself maturing and getting a little bit wiser, you're not afraid of being who you are."

—BARBARA STREISAND, singer, actress, director, and producer

Mirabella magazine

OCTOBER 26, 1947

ATTORNEY AND

FIRST LADY

courtesy of The White House

27

Other First Ladies may have greeted the fifty-year mark with all the enthusiasm of a root canal. Not Hillary Rodham Clinton. For three days, she reveled in an ongoing celebration that shuttled from Washington to Chicago, involved hundreds of well-wishers, a dozen cakes, and countless choruses of "Happy Birthday."
But the best part was being back in her hometown of Park Ridge, Illinois, an upper-middle-class suburb, where she was feted by her girlhood friends. We are familiar with Hillary as a wife, mother, lawyer, author, and behind-the-scenes force. But to see her surrounded by women with whom she shares

"I've had more women tell me they feel an incredible burst of energy . . ."

the same history was to understand how she keeps her balance.

Eavesdropping on this group as they sat in the pint-sized furniture of their old elementary school was to stroll down our own Memory Lanes. They reminisced about growing up in a time of innocence, when kids still went home for lunch and the wrong kind of hosiery could get you labeled "too fast." (Hillary petitioned her dad to allow her to wear "nylons" to her sixth-grade dance, but he wouldn't budge and the dreaded white anklets remained.)

"It was a time when we had the freedom to go trick-or-treating at every single house—except maybe for one place, where some real old lady lived," said Hillary.

"Yeah," remarked one pal dryly. "She was probably fifty."

But for all the good-natured jokes, there was an easy rapport that came from accomplishment; from being among the first wave of women to benefit from expanded opportunities. "There was no distinction between me and my brothers or any barriers thrown up to me," Hillary often says.

She proved that over and over: first at Wellesley College, where she delivered a feisty commencement speech denouncing corporate greed; then, as one of only thirty women accepted into Yale Law School's class of 1972, where she caught the eye of an ambitious young man from Arkansas. ("I just had never met anybody like that," she said. Most remarkably, she noted, "he wasn't afraid of me.")

However, while the level playing field qualified her for a meatier role than her predecessors', it also opened her to more criticism. "Men my age and older don't like her," said one acquaintance. "They don't want their wives to be like her, but they do want their daughters to be."

Since moving into the White House she has also weathered her

28

"*It's a time to think about your calling, your passions.*"

share of personal setbacks: the deaths of her father and mother-in-law, and a dear friend's suicide. Now, having coped with an empty nest ("I told Chelsea she can always come home"), she has emerged stronger, more resilient, and ready to leave her mark.

"I've had more women tell me they feel an incredible burst of energy," she told Oprah Winfrey the morning after her big birthday bash in Chicago. "It's a time to think about your calling, your passions."

Whether that will be welfare, children's issues, or something else, she is eager to tackle the next passage. But for now, her best contribution may be that she made this once-matronly milestone downright chic, as evidenced by the sentiment Oprah penned in her birthday book: "You're making 50 look like the place to be. Can't wait to join you!"

       ❋   ❋   ❋

29

I wish I knew the value of every single day. I have fifty years behind me and I honestly don't know where they all went.

I know the importance of hanging tough, of persevering. I was always taught those lessons of hanging on for dear life—and they've served me well.

When I was at my elementary school, visiting with my old friends and teachers, it struck me: I wish I had been a little more patient . . . I wish I had not been so hard on myself and others.

JANE CURTIN

SEPTEMBER 6, 1947
ACTRESS

© Alan Levenson

30

As one of the original cast members of Saturday Night Live, *Jane Curtin became part of a national phenomenon.*

Even though she was on the show for only five years (1975–1980), the impact made it seem much longer. Curtin subsequently starred in two other successful TV series, but to baby boomers she will always be the anchor on "Weekend Update" or the matriarch of the Conehead clan or the mother to Lisa Loopner, ready to whip up egg salad sandwiches at a moment's notice.

Born and raised in Cambridge, Massachusetts, Curtin studied drama at Northeastern University, but dropped out in 1968 to pursue acting full-time. She joined an improvisational troupe for four years (which performed in a Boston garage) before heading to New York. After several years of rejection and unemployment, she landed the role as one of the Not Ready for Prime Time Players during the golden years of SNL.

That was followed with a five-year stint in Kate & Allie, *for which she twice earned Emmys for her portrayal of an affable divorcee. Then came the ill-fated* Working It Out, *in 1990, followed by a hiatus from series TV, until 1996, when* 3rd Rock from the Sun *became a huge hit for NBC.*

Curtin and producer Patrick Lynch have a thirteen-year-old daughter, Tess, and live in California.

* * *

I've learned that it is important to keep in contact with children . . . to have some sort of connection with them because they keep you in touch with the world. You don't have to have your own, but you should find a way to talk with them, to be around them, just don't ignore them.

I look at my friends who have no contact with kids and they're out of the loop. They become selfish, self-absorbed, and cranky. Because of my daughter, I have an idea of what is going on in pop culture that I wouldn't otherwise have. If you listen and pay attention to kids, you have some kind of inkling to what this next generation will create, which is a very exhilarating prospect.

I was fortunate to have someone pay that kind of attention to me. My mother, who graduated from Radcliffe in 1935, was in a class made up of extraordinary

"With age, the work is primary and the ego is secondary."

women, who overcame tremendous odds to go to college. We used to attend her reunions and they were all doing fascinating things, like living in deplorable conditions with their own kids while changing the library system of Chad, or something like that. So growing up in that kind of environment, I always knew anything was possible. The more you do, the more things happen.

Rejection is part of the deal of being an actress, but it's also part of life. Rejection is how I learned what I was cut out to do—it always narrows your focus. If you're foolish enough to ask why you were rejected at an audition, you're told. I've been told "Because you have gray teeth" or "Because your face is too big." So my other piece of advice is that when you're rejected, it's better not to ask why.

As you get older, achievement is still important, but you're not quite so driven. What I do for a living is pretend, so the goal becomes trying to have as much fun as you can—and when the cast is having fun, the audience can sense that. My mother taught me that nothing was so insurmountable that you couldn't laugh at it.

Saturday Night Live certainly made me more visible. It helps, it hurts, it changes your life completely. But it's different this time around [with *3rd Rock from the Sun*]. With age, the work is primary and the ego is secondary. Really all I wanted was to keep working. Becoming "a name" was never part of the plan.

Would I want this kind of life for my daughter? I think she'd have a ball—she's smart enough and sophisticated enough to know what's real and what's not. What more could you wish for your child than to have interesting work?

FAYE DUNAWAY

JANUARY 14, 1941
ACTRESS

© Charles Busch

It has been thirty years since she blew audiences away in Bonnie and Clyde, *in a role that launched a career as well as a fashion trend.*

But while Faye Dunaway carved out a niche as a renegade, she was really closer to the screen sirens of earlier eras—like Grace Kelly and Greta Garbo. Go beyond the exterior layer of glamour and you'll find an unsettling cool at the center. Perhaps the secret lies somewhere in her Florida panhandle roots.

With more than forty films to her credit, Dunaway has played some of the meatiest roles Hollywood had to offer. Besides Bonnie Parker, she was the tragic Evelyn Mulwray in the classic Roman Polanski film Chinatown *and the snakey TV executive Diana Christensen in* Network, *which earned her a Best Actress Oscar in 1976.*

Her career chugged along until 1981, when she decided to play Joan Crawford in Mommie Dearest, *which she calls "the turning point in my career."*

In one blow, she was reduced to campy icon. The public had trouble discerning where Crawford ended and Dunaway began. The experience was so painful that any mention of the film is deleted from her official biography, despite the fact that many critics praised it as among her best work.

The portrayal set off a patch of what Dunaway calls "bad luck"—a failed CBS series, It Had to Be You, *and a feud with Andrew Lloyd Webber, who fired her from the role of Norma Desmond in the musical* Sunset Boulevard.

But life took an upturn in 1994, with an Emmy for her performance in a Columbo *episode. The next year brought favorable reviews for her performance as Marlon Brando's wife in* Don Juan DeMarco, *and an autobiography,* Looking for Gatsby, *and Dunaway was very much back in business. In 1996, she starred in a trio of movies (*The Chamber, Albino Alligator, *and* Drunks*).*

Dunaway, though, is not waiting for Hollywood to come calling. She formed her own production company and one of her first projects will be playing the opera diva Maria Callas in the national tour of Master Class.

"It's about what you can do each day to achieve your dreams."

She has been married twice—to Peter Wolf (formerly of the J. Geils Band) and celebrity photographer Terry O'Neill, whom she divorced in 1986. She resides in Los Angeles and New York with her sixteen-year-old son, Liam O'Neill.

*   *   *

It's really about self-reliance. Nobody is going to read your mind, no man is going to do it for you, no one is going to be as vigilant. There are no Gatsbys. If you're smart, you'll start developing your own material right away. You look ahead . . . and start doing it now when you have some power. You need to be proactive in your career and if there is no good material, find your own. There is a way to put properties together, to function as a producer, and if you can't find financial backing here, go to Europe with foreign pre-sales.

It's not a question of what other people currently think about you. It's about what you can do each day to achieve your dreams.

35

SANDY DUNCAN

FEBRUARY 20, 1946
ACTRESS

Ever since she climbed onto the stage during a dance recital at age four, the adjective "sunny" has stuck to Sandy Duncan like flypaper. Yet her life has certainly had its dark moments.

© Robert Vance Blosser

Her TV series Funny Face— *one of the hits of the 1971–1972 season—ended abruptly when a fibroid tumor cost her the sight in her left eye. After she recovered, Duncan returned to a revamped format, only to see the show falter in the ratings. More recently, she has battled a depression that "was like falling into a black hole for two years."*

Duncan, a native of East Texas, experienced a childhood that was devoted to the study of tap, ballet, and acrobatic dancing. A self-confessed approval junkie, she was "either hysterical with joy from her [teacher's] praise or hysterical with despair because of her criticism."

After making the rounds of Dallas summer stock and dinner theaters, she moved to New York at age eighteen for a part in The Music Man. *Four years later, she garnered a Tony nomination for* Canterbury Tales, *a feat she repeated in 1979 with* Peter Pan. *The children's musical was roundly praised by the critics,* Newsweek *gushing that it could run "for as long as there are kids in New York."*

*In between, there were films (*Star Spangled Girl*) and numerous TV appearances, including* Roots, *the landmark miniseries, and* Funny Face, *both of which brought her Emmy nominations.*

The 1980s and 1990s have been more low-profile, mostly concert dates, short-run theater productions, and writing, all of which are more compatible with parenting. She and her third husband, Don Correia, and their two teenage sons live in New York, where her Chinaberry Production Company is based.

"The more you learn how to use the ups and the downs, the easier it is to come to some real growth."

* * *

Anytime there's a choice between my career and my kids, my career always comes second. I've passed on a lot of shows because I didn't want to be away for long periods of time—and then saw them go on to be huge hits, like [the Broadway musical] *Chicago*. The producers came to me first, but I just couldn't see being out of town for nine months.

The star thing doesn't interest me at all. The few times where I was in a very high profile situation, I didn't like it. But what does interest me is the work, the process.

It would have been easier if I had either thrown myself into [my career] or stopped working completely. It's finding that middle ground that's the toughest because when you're doing one thing, you are torn by the other. The trick is to stay with work just enough . . . so it's always on a back burner.

My advice is to remember that you cannot have it all ways. Don't use [parenthood] as a scapegoat; this was your choice . . . and if you voluntarily make a choice, well, then you have to stick with it. Also, don't define yourself by other people's terms. Not too long ago a woman came up to me and said, "Oh, you're Sandy Duncan? I just loved you when you used to be big." It doesn't really bother me—perhaps because of all the things I've done, parenthood still feels the most important.

A few years ago, I went through a two-year clinical depression. For a long time, I kept the balls up in the air for a lot of people and it just wore me out. It was as if this alabaster shell just cracked. It's very frightening . . . I didn't know what to do. Should I just take some Prozac and get back up on the horse? But I don't think that's the answer; it's just something I had to work through and I'm glad I did, because I'm much more comfortable in my skin now.

A lot of people choose to keep the blinders on and keep chugging along in this rut and it's not a very healthy way to live. The more you learn how to use the ups and the downs, the easier it is to come to some real growth.

LINDA ELLERBEE

© Gittings/Skipworth, Inc.

AUGUST 15, 1945
BROADCAST JOURNALIST

The irreverent Linda Ellerbee has gone from small Houston TV station to big-time broadcaster for all three major networks. It was on NBC's Overnight *that she attracted a cult following among insomniacs who were drawn to her intelligent writing and wry wit. (Her signature sign-off: "And so it goes.")*

In 1986, she formed her own TV production company, called Lucky Duck Productions, with partner Rolfe Tessem. The company was started on a shoestring budget with one employee. Today, Lucky Duck has a staff of twenty-five and is best known for Nick News, *an award-winning news and documentary series for children, which Ellerbee also writes and hosts. In between, she has married four times (in one decade, no less), had two kids, and battled alcoholism and breast cancer, managing to excavate humor and insight even from life's lowest moments.*

In one often repeated anecdote that she is quick to confirm, Ellerbee was playing catch with her golden retriever, when she bent over to pick up the ball and her prosthesis fell out. The dog, figuring that this was just part of the game, took off with it, followed by Ellerbee chasing him down the road yelling, "Come back with my breast."

And so it goes.

All changes are a risk—and it does get harder as you get older—but change makes you know you're alive. You're exploring, you're stumbling—almost certainly stumbling if my past is any indication—but there is a certain exhilaration, too. You can't wait to see what happens next.

Of course, there are the changes we choose and then there are the changes that choose us. I chose to leave the network, but breast cancer chose me. What I like most about change is that it's a synonym for "hope." If you are taking a risk, what you are really saying is "I believe in tomorrow and I will be part of it."

I have trouble understanding the fear people have about change and certainly about aging. Our prospects haven't narrowed just because the years have; if anything, they've never been richer. Oh, I suppose I'll never be a brain surgeon, but there is so much time left for new choices, for new paths. At fifty, you can have another half century left.

We are already rewriting the definition of "old." My goodness, there are women in their fifties with children under ten. We're hiking, we're writing plays, we're running for office, we're quitting

"What I like most about change is that it's a synonym for 'hope.'"

salaried jobs to open our own businesses—and what's so amazing is that we're doing it for the first time at this age.

Our notion of retirement will be totally different than the generation before us. We women in our fifties do not have a lot in common with women in their seventies, and a generation ago, I don't think that was the case.

All I know is that I can take the four flights of stairs in my house better today than I could five years ago. I'm taking active vacations—something I wouldn't have even considered when I was younger. I just returned from white-water canoeing in Montana, and next fall I'm hiking through England by myself. Those are the things that will keep us young . . . that will keep us engaged.

NORA EPHRON

MAY 19, 1941
WRITER AND DIRECTOR

© Michael O'Neill

In a perfect world, we'd all have girlfriends like Nora Ephron: smart, honest, and, above all, witty—even when life becomes painfully complex.

*Whether on the page or on the screen, she's at her best when she's mining material from her own life: divorce (*Heartburn*), the tug-of-war between work and motherhood (*This Is My Life*), and the search for our true soul mate (*Sleepless in Seattle*). How did she know that it mirrors our life, too?*

*Tapping into universal pain is a skill she learned at an early age. Her parents, Phoebe and Henry Ephron, were screenwriters during the mid-1960s (*Take Her, She's Mine; Carousel*). Whenever she fretted about breast size or a prom date, they preached that "everything is copy."*

After graduating from Wellesley College in 1962, she landed a reporting job at the New York Post. *Since magazines paid more, she went off to* Esquire *and* New York *and penned two successful* collections of essays (Crazy Salad and Scribble Scribble).

But it was really 1983's Heartburn—a thinly veiled account of her failed marriage to Washington Post reporter (and father of her two sons) Carl Bernstein—that made her a Hollywood player.

"I feel very lucky at my age because I'm married to the person I should have married in the first place..."

That same year, Ephron branched out into screenwriting with the drama Silkwood. Her first effort (co-written with Alice Arlen) brought her an Academy Award nomination for best original screenplay. Two more nominations followed with two romantic— and phenomenally successful—comedies, When Harry Met Sally and Sleepless in Seattle (which she also directed). Other directing credits include This Is My Life, Mixed Nuts, and Michael, co-written with her sister Delia, "because we share about 60 percent of a brain."

Ephron lives with her third husband, writer Nicholas Pileggi (Wiseguys), and her two teenage sons in New York.

•   •   •

I don't [write about myself] anymore, but it is a very useful coping mechanism. In some kind of deep and stupid way, it forces you to come to terms with things. Joan Didion said she wrote to find out how she felt and I think there's a lot of truth to that.

Certainly, Heartburn was the most autobiographical of all my work. It's a comic monologue that shows you can take something very painful in your life and make it into a funny story, if you can just figure out how. Even if I hadn't written it, I'd still recommend it to anyone going through a divorce.

I didn't want anything to do with the movie business, but after my marriage broke up, I didn't have enough money to stay in journalism, so that's how I ended up here. I wrote screenplays that didn't get made, then I made ones that did get made and when that happens, it changes your view in a dramatic way.

My advice to anyone wanting to become a screenwriter is: Know something. I see these twenty-one-year-olds wanting to get in the movie business and how much life can they possibly know? I had written for newspapers and magazines for years [before I stepped on a set] so I knew stuff. And I had been married so many times that I even knew a little bit about that.

I feel very lucky at my age because I'm married to the person I should have married in the first place, but other than that you have to be crazy to think that it's fun to get older. It irritates me to read all these Pollyannaish things about life after menopause. It is not pleasant to look in the mirror and watch the inevitable decline of skin tone. No matter how you feel right now about your looks, in a few years you will wish you looked that way. I never wore a bikini— now, I wish I had worn a bikini when I was in my twenties. What a waste that I didn't have one on at all times.

JANE FONDA

DECEMBER 21, 1937
ACTRESS

© Firooz Zahedi

One of the most luminous stars of our time, Jane Fonda has shown incredible staying power. Perhaps that's because, over the years, she has worn several personas.

45

From 1960s Hollywood starlet to 1970s antiwar activist to 1980s exercise guru to 1990s corporate wife, Fonda has managed to keep us intrigued.

In recent years, Fonda has studiously avoided the limelight. Retired from acting since her 1991 marriage to media mogul Ted Turner, she can be seen at Atlanta Braves games (her husband owns the team), but is rarely heard. She has spoken out only to promote her cookbook (Jane Fonda Cooking for Healthy Living) and her favorite cause, the Georgia Campaign for Adolescent Pregnancy Prevention (GCAPP), which she helped create with Turner Foundation funds.

This lower profile is a dramatic shift for the actress whose name has been synomous with activism. (Her opposition to the Vietnam war earned her the animosity of veterans' groups and a spot on the

Nixon administration's enemies list.) Or for someone who was everywhere, urging us "to go for the burn." (Her workout tape remained a best-seller for almost five years and is credited with single-handedly transforming the home video industry

While the personas come and go, her films endure. Her most celebrated roles—for which she won two Academy Awards—were Klute *(1971) and* Coming Home *(1978). But, even if you delete these from her résumé, Fonda's body of work would still be the envy of most actresses:* Julia, China Syndrome, *and* On Golden Pond, *which was the only time she appeared on-screen with her father, Henry Fonda. (It also brought him his first Best Actor Oscar, just four months before he died.)*

Now her top priority is her third marriage (her previous husbands were French director Roger Vadim and California assemblyman Tom Hayden). She has two grown children.

46

·   ·   ·

My life feels more and more like a trail of clues, like Hansel and Gretel's bread crumbs dropped along the path, beckoning me to retrace my steps and learn from where I am and where I might go.

One of the things that maturity has brought is the revelation that all along I've been heading to where I was at the start, reminding me of the phrase I first heard in eighth-grade French class, incomprehensible at the time: *Plus ça change, plus c'est la même chose* (the more it changes, the more it stays the same).

My life has been one of continual redefinition, with each chapter seeming to have little connection to the one before. I can now see however that within each phase is a thread of continuity and leitmotif of

"One of the things that maturity has brought is the revelation that all along I've been

growth and strength. I have changed so much, yet I am the same.

Discovering this continuity of strength has been hard for me, covered over by so many layers of wanting to please, of "I'm not good enough or smart enough or lovable enough."

This has been an empowering discovery and has led me to another revelation. For years, I've been saying that the only thing that I have never had was a truly intimate relationship. To myself, I wondered if I was even capable.

I've been an exemplary caregiver during periods of my life, mistaking this for intimacy, not realizing that it's possible to give enormously to another yet leave yourself behind, not realizing that there can be no true intimacy unless you show up, all of you, 100 percent. I'd always felt that it would be a sign of selfishness to explore and express my own feelings and needs. Often I would blame signifcant others for lack of intimacy in our relationship.

If you've grown up not knowing intimacy, the vulnerability of opening your heart fully and deeply to another is terrifying, but at a point in my fifties, I realized that either I had to shut up about wanting intimacy and settle for my habitual comfort level or I had to step up to the plate, bite the bullet, hold my nose, take a deep breath, and plunge. Wow! Scary! Harder than any challenge I've ever faced in my life and I've faced many. But what I'm learning (and it is a lesson I don't think I could have learned in my earlier years—or middle ones, for that matter) is that intimacy can be learned; I am capable of showing up, heart and soul. You need courage, determination, humor, and a willing, patient partner. I expect to continue learning about intimacy and discovering more bread crumbs along life's path until the day I die, and if I do, I'll go out a lucky, happy, and yes, a strong woman.

heading to where I was at the start . . . I have changed so much, yet I am the same."

"Surely the consolation prize of age is in finding out how few things are worth worrying over, and how many things that we once desired, we don't want anymore."

—DOROTHY DIX, journalist

The Wit & Wisdom of Women

NANCY FRIDAY

AUGUST 27, 1938
WRITER

For a quarter century, Nancy Friday has been one of our most astute observers of women and sexuality.

In this tell-all era, it's hard to remember that there was a time when nice people didn't talk about mothers and erotic experiences in the same sentence. Friday changed all that in 1978 with My Mother, My Self, *which went on to become an international best-seller.*

It isn't only her zest in diving into taboo topics, but her candor that has earned her a place in the firmament. Inviting us along on her own personal odyssey, she serves as in inimitable tour guide, regardless of the subject. In her latest book, The Power of Beauty—*part self-therapy, part cultural memoir—she recalls the bended-knee posture she mastered during her adolescence, "the art of being less"—as she called it—and in one fell swoop, we are trans-*

ported back to the lunch tables, locker rooms, and dances of our own awkward youth.

Friday was raised in the South—Charleston, South Carolina—in the 1950s, where being gawky was the equivalent of being invisible. Life improved immeasurably when she went off to Wellesley College, briefly edited a travel magazine, and then began writing books, including My Secret Garden *(on sexual fantasies) and* Jealousy. *But it never seemed enough. "Neither professional success, great friends, nor the love of men could recapture the self-confidence . . . I owned before I lost myself in the external mirrors of adolescence."*

Friday and her second husband, Norman Pearlstine—editor-in-chief of Time*—split their time between Connecticut and Key West.*

• • •

What have I learned? When we were younger, we knew what popular culture taught us—or what we saw in our mothers. But as the first generation to rewrite the rules, we needed to relearn things. Take, for example, something as simple as our voices. I remember the first time I heard Barbara Jordan speak with this rolling, thunderous voice. It made quite an impression on me because women had always had little voices, both politically and vocally. Now, there are so many women who speak well and in rich paragraphs. This is something that could only have come with time.

I know the keys and sources of my tension. You've got to understand the buried anxieties and rages if you are to have a great and long life—and then you need to let it go. If you didn't have a perfect relationship with your mother, then get over it. A baby, a little girl needs a perfect mommy, but you don't. If you're still angry about brothers and sisters who got more than you—or so you thought—then put it aside. It only holds you back. Old jealousies and resentments within the family age us far more than the sun. If you don't let go of those demons—they will pull you down, far more than gravity. You will look ill and haggard long before your time.

"If people know that you see them . . . that you hear them, that you really are taking them in, then you will never be without friends."

Steer clear of people who are envious—it's the one emotion of which nothing good can be said. It's destructive, mean-spirited, and petty. We live in the age of envy and so much of it is over surface appearance. When was the last time you heard someone point out another person's honesty? Integrity? Goodness? That's why so many people are starved to be looked at. We live in the age of the empty package.

What everyone is really starved for is content. This third act—from age fifty on—can be the best act. If people know that you see them . . . that you hear them, that you really are taking them in, then you will never be without friends.

51

ANNETTE FUNICELLO

OCTOBER 22, 1942
ACTRESS

52

If you were a girl in the 1950s, you wanted to be just like her. On Walt Disney's The Mickey Mouse Club, *there were lots of singers and dancers, but only one star: a dark-eyed, dimpled teen known simply as Annette.*

If anyone led a charmed life, it was Annette. She was discovered when Disney came to see a performance of Swan Lake *at a dance school recital. Actually, he had come to see the conductor, but was enchanted by the dark-haired girl dancing in the front row. As luck would have it, Disney had one last spot to fill in his ensemble of Mouseketeers.*

courtesy of The Walt Disney Company

Even after she hung up her mouse ears, she was never out of the spotlight—first in a wave of beach party movies (where she never exposed her navel), then pitching peanut butter. The likable straight arrow, she went from every girl's best friend to every boy's dream date to every kid's perfect mom.

Indeed, in real life, she was devoted to raising her three children, now adults. Married in 1965 to talent agent Jack Gilardi (whom she divorced in 1982), she lives in Encino, California, with her second husband, racehorse breeder Glen Holt.

Divorce aside, she still seemed the perennial fairy-tale princess. But in 1987, she first started experiencing symptoms—blurred vision and loss of balance—of multiple sclerosis (MS). When she couldn't hide the degenerative nerve disease any longer, she revealed her condition in 1992. "I'm so happy not to hide anymore," she said at the time. "I didn't go public for a long time because I believed people wanted to think that nothing bad ever happened to Annette."

She now serves as a spokesperson for the National Multiple Sclerosis Society. Because speaking had become so difficult, Annette wrote her "wisdom."

* * *

Since I've had MS, I have had to look much differently at everything. I certainly appreciate the values of life, especially my family, which is most important. Also, my fans that have expressed their deep affection for me for so many years was something I could never quite grasp. Now, through their prayers and the thousands of letters and cards that they've sent, that love has overwhelmed me. It does my heart and my spirit good.

Probably the greatest lesson I've learned in life is: Don't take anything for granted. The small pleasures of life are worth everything. You must live each day to its fullest.

PHYLLIS GEORGE

JUNE 25, 1949
BROADCASTER AND ENTREPRENEUR

If one word could sum up Phyllis George's career, it would be "eclectic." Few people can boast that they have been on the cover of both People *and* Poultry Processing.

54

George has been in the spotlight since winning the title of Miss America in 1971. Four years later, she became the first woman sportscaster, co-anchoring NFL Today *on CBS, where she held her own with veterans Brent Musberger and Irv Cross.*

But she landed her biggest role in 1979, when she married Kentucky businessman John Y. Brown, Jr., who announced his candidacy for governor right after their honeymoon. When he was elected, many residents didn't expect much from the new first lady— especially since she shuttled between Kentucky and New York for her broadcasting job—but, once again, she won them over.

Indeed, it took a transplanted Texan to see the beauty in the handmade quilts, baskets, furniture, and other crafts so plentiful in the Bluegrass State. George (she has dropped her husband's sur-name) became an advocate for the artisans, establishing the Kentucky Art & Craft Foundation and penning two books on the subject.

Her next challenge was more painful. From almost the moment she was hired as co-host of the CBS Morning News *in 1985, George faced a barrage of criticism. Despite her earlier success on* NFL Today, *she was doomed by her lack of hard-news credentials. (Remember her suggesting a hug between Cathleen Crowell Webb and accused rapist Gary Dotson?) Eight months later, she and CBS parted company.*

Returning to Kentucky, she entered her "mompreneur" period, starting a company called Chicken by George, which she later sold to Hormel Foods (she is still chairwoman). She also continues to work in broadcasting—but this time, it's the Nashville Network and QVC.

In 1996, after seventeen years of marriage, she filed for divorce from Brown. She currently splits her time between her Kentucky farm and New York City, where she resides with her two teenage children, Lincoln and Pamela.

*   *   *

I just lost my father, which has left a huge void in my life. I think about how my dad always knew how to make a child feel special and secure—even if that "kid" is in her forties. People from back home in Denton, Texas, would say to me, "Your dad is just so proud of you." He'd go around asking people, "Did you see who she interviewed?" or "Have you heard about her chicken company?" and it still felt so good. My self-esteem has been high because of what my parents gave me . . . and I hope I can do the same for my children.

I long for them to have roots, that same sense of belonging to a place that I had growing up in Denton.

I've always been very focused. I entered the [Miss America] pageant because I saw it as a stepping-stone out of my small town and for scholarship money. But would I want it for my daughter? No, there are many more opportunities today for young women. But it would always be her choice.

It's more important for young women to be valued for what they accomplish rather than what they look like. I remember when I was on *NFL Today* no one worked harder, traveled more, or was better prepared for interviews. It was very frustrating because it was only the "beauty thing" that people saw.

Over the years, I've learned to do what I want to do and not what other people want me to do. When I was younger, I was so busy pleasing everyone and achieving so much that it was easy to neglect my spiritual and emotional self. So I've learned to say no more—although it's a constant battle not to fall back into my old traps.

I am better at recognizing what's a good fit and what's not. When I took the *CBS Morning News* job, the network promised they would tailor it to me, to my style . . . but it didn't happen that way. I had found my niche—which is personality journalism—and that's what they told me they wanted, but it wasn't what they wanted at all. I was so unhappy—I was like a fish out of water in hard news. But even that was a great learning experience because I found out what I didn't want to do.

So I got off the treadmill; I went home to be with my children and I loved it . . . the piano and dance recitals, the soccer and baseball games. Barbara Walters once advised me to enjoy them while they're young or I would regret it later and she was right.

"Over the years, I've learned to do what I want to do and not what other people want me to do."

I know that you have to be a self-starter. You can't wait for someone else to start your engine. An optimist sees opportunity in every difficulty, while a pessimist sees difficulty in every opportunity.

Find a void and fill it—that's what I did when I came up with the idea of boneless, marinated chicken. There is always more than one way to do everything, which tends to make some corporate people nervous. But you've got to give a little and take a little on almost everything. Do whatever you have to do, but don't break up the game.

ELLEN GOODMAN

58

© Kim Arrington

Before there was Anna Quindlen or Maureen Dowd, there was Ellen Goodman.

Since 1976, when her Boston Globe *column was first syndicated, Goodman's ability to cut through complex, muddled issues with insight and common sense has earned her a loyal national following. Today, her "At Large" column appears on op-ed pages of some 450 newspapers across the country.*

After graduating from Radcliffe College in 1963, she worked for Newsweek *magazine and the* Detroit Free Press *before being hired at the* Globe *in 1967. In 1973, she spent a year at Harvard as a prestigious Neiman Fellow. Seven years later, she received the Pulitzer Prize for Distinguished Commentary, journalism's highest honor.*

In addition, her work has appeared in numerous magazines, including Ms. *and* Life. *Her book on social change,* Turning Points, *was pub-*

"As you age, this business of living becomes simpler—like

lished in 1979. Five collections of her columns have also been published; the most recent is Value Judgments, *which came out in 1993. Goodman and her husband live in Brookline, Massachusetts.*

*   *   *

Probably the most important skill you learn is how to listen.

As you get older, I think you're humbled and you certainly don't judge as much as you do when you're younger. Perhaps that's because you don't make it to fifty without having had your head handed to you.

You try not to envy others because—more than once—you've seen people who looked like they had everything and then, only later, found out that they have lost a child to cancer or have a parent with Alzheimer's disease.

It's the difference between being a sprinter versus a long-distance runner. So, as you age, this business of living becomes simpler—like just doing good work, taking care of the people you love.

I think the reason so many of us start playing golf as we get older—aside from the fact that our poor bodies can't take two hours of tennis anymore—is that it's a wonderful metaphor for life.

In golf, you're always recovering . . . always playing it as it lays. You can blow one hole and make it up on the next one. It's all about how to come back, which is probably one of the most important character traits you can have.

You can't do this job and be too much of a perfectionist. Some days, you just have to go with what you've got and that, too, applies to life. Most people hate to make mistakes, but it happens. Give yourself a break. That's why God made erasers.

just doing good work, taking care of the people you love."

fifty on fifty

We all want to be the perfect mom, the perfect spouse, the perfect worker, but if you're juggling a lot of balls, you're going to drop one from time to time. When my daughter was in college, I named the ten worst things I ever did to her and she did the same thing and our lists didn't match at all. That tells you a lot right there. Besides, I used to have an expression with her: It's all going to come out in therapy, anyway.

So, to me, resiliency is the big issue in life. We're all going to get knocked around. By the time you reach fifty, you know how resilient you are—and that's a big deal. It's not about avoiding the rough spots, but recovering from them.

SUE GRAFTON

© Michael Goldman

She began her popular alphabet series with A Is for Alibi *in 1982. Fourteen books (and letters) later, it's* N Is for Noose. *She plans to reach the end of the alphabet by 2020, with* Z is for Zero.

Sue Grafton has become a force in publishing by giving women a protagonist they can relate to— namely Kinsey Millhone, a tough-minded, twice- divorced female detective, who lives in Santa Teresa, the pseudonym for her home base in Santa Barbara.

A Kentucky native, Grafton had parents who were both alcoholics, who, ironically, she credits for her success. "One of my theories is that no one with a happy childhood ever amounts to much in this world," she said. "They're so well adjusted, they're never driven to achieve anything."

Drive is something Grafton has in spades. Even though her career as a writer began in the late 1960s, with her novel Keziah Dane, *it took another decade to build up the kind of nest egg that would allow her to break away from her day job in TV writing.*

Kinsey Millhone first sprung to life out of the ashes of Grafton's

61

own bitter divorce and custody battle. To counter her feelings of powerlessness, she harbored homicidal fantasies—specifically, sneaking poisonous oleander into her ex's allergy capsules. The plot moved seamlessly from her head to the printed page and Millhone was born, solving new mysteries at the rate of one a year.

She is married to Steve Humphrey, a philosophy professor, and has three adult children and two grandchildren.

· · ·

I am terrified of failing, particularly as the alphabet proceeds. I can just hear the critics sharpening their knives, waiting for me to fall flat on my face. I have gotten better at telling myself, "So you screw up . . . so what's the big deal? God will still let you breathe." I've always felt that fear makes you cautious, conservative, and bland. It keeps you on the safe road, which is never a very interesting road.

> "Train yourself to listen to that small voice that tells us what's important and what's not."

To me, persistence is the lesson. When you're twenty, passion gives you the energy and propels you forward, but in your fifties, passion is too unpredictable, too erratic. Persistence, though, is always available, no matter the age.

My first three manuscripts were rejected. Then, in 1967, I wrote *Keziah Dane* [about a Depression-era widow], the next book [*The Lolly-Madonna War*] was published only in England, and then my next two manuscripts were rejected. The eighth one was *A Is for Alibi*. So breaking in is no guarantee. In fact, that's when your work is just beginning. I like to help new writers, but only the ones who understand how hard it is. Too many are focused on publication and the best-seller list and not enough are focused on writing well.

Too many people stop learning. [To give her books an authoritative tone, Grafton immerses herself in such esoteric subjects as ballistics and toxicology.] Kinsey can only know what I know.

I just started lifting weights, which was something I knew nothing about. It's just a hoot to be such a novice at something . . . then, purely through your own efforts and persistence, you can change the way your body looks. I find that amazing.

So many women have a poor body image—they sit around eating cookies and wondering where they went astray. I say, "Put down the cookies and come to my home gym and we will kick some butt." But you've got to be into it. Whatever you do, you have to love the process, not because it's fun or pleasurable, but because it's hard to do.

Here's what I try to work on with myself. The first: to keep ego out of the way as much as possible. Once you have a little bit of success, it's easy for your head to start swelling. You become self-conscious and see yourself as being much more important than you really are. To write well, you have to totally give up ego.

The second is to listen to self. The world is forever plucking at us, draining away time, attention, energy. So train yourself to listen to that small voice that tells us what's important and what's not.

63

MARION HAMMER

APRIL 26, 1939
FORMER PRESIDENT, NATIONAL RIFLE ASSOCIATION

64

© Michael Ives @ National Rifle Association

When she was named president of the National Rifle Association of America, Marion Hammer became the first woman to ever hold that position in the organization's 125-year history.

She ascended to the top spot in 1995, when her predecessor suffered a heart attack while deer hunting. Some cynics saw the appointment of Hammer, a grandmother, as a ploy to soften the NRA's image.

But one glance at Hammer's résumé and it's clear that her pistol-packing credentials are impeccable.

She fired her first shot at age five and won a shelfful of marksmanship awards. Her political awakening didn't come until later—1968, to be exact—when Congress passed the first major federal gun control law in fifty years. Since then, she has been one of the gun lobby's most outspoken advocates.

The high point of her career came in 1987, when she helped convince the Florida legislature to pass a bill allowing residents to carry concealed, registered guns. It was enough to earn her the NRA's Activist/Lobbyist of the Year Award and the Roy Rogers Man of the Year Award.

She was taught to shoot by her grandfather, who managed to drive the point home quite vividly: If Hammer bagged a squirrel, he bought the next box of shells; but if she came home empty-handed, the ammunition came out of her own pocket.

Divorced since 1980, she has three grown daughters and three grandchildren. She lives in Tallahassee, Florida.

•　•　•

You will never succeed if you try to please too many people or stand in the middle of the road. My grandfather taught me that a person of principle will never compromise and warned me that there is nothing in the middle of the road but a yellow stripe and dead possum.

Today, I try to analyze things quickly and fairly. People who are reluctant to make decisions and take responsibility for them are generally not happy.

Criticism goes with the territory. If you're going to take a position and stand for your beliefs, then you have to accept that all people will not share those beliefs. Whether they have enough information, of course, is another issue.

The way I view criticism is that it is really born of frustration. They don't understand you and you don't understand them. I don't try to change people's minds, but I do give them accurate information so they have the tools to make correct and valid decisions.

It's easy to be against something you know nothing about—just as it's easy to kill a piece of legislation. But it's hard to pass a good

"Have the confidence to believe in what you're doing."

65

bill because that requires understanding and effort and knowledge. People routinely just say no so they don't have to be bothered; they don't have to look for real solutions.

My grandfather taught me that if you're trying to get from one side of the woods to the other and the wolves are snapping at your heels, if you keep stopping and kick at the wolves, you'll never get out of the woods. So don't get distracted by your critics. Complete your task. And, above all, have the confidence to believe in what you're doing.

VALERIE HARPER

AUGUST 22, 1940
ACTRESS

courtesy of Valerie Harper

It was Rhoda Morgenstern—the most beloved neighbor since Ethel Mertz—that made Valerie Harper a household name, first on The Mary Tyler Moore Show *and then on her own spin-off series. When* Rhoda *premiered on September 9, 1974, it captured the top spot in the Nielsen ratings with its very first broadcast—a feat that had never been accomplished before or duplicated since. Her nine-year stint also brought Harper a shelfful of accolades, from the Emmy (four times) to Harvard University's Hasty Pudding Award.*

The daughter of a salesman, Harper was born in Suffern, New York, and attended Hunter College and made her stage debut at Radio City Music Hall in the corps de ballet. Since then, her credits include Broadway (the Tony Award–winning Story Theatre*) and film (she met her husband, Tony Cacciotti, a personal trainer, in*

67

fifty on fifty

1979, when he whipped her into shape for a swimsuit scene in Neil Simon's Chapter Two).

Most recently, the two collaborated on The Dragon and the Pearl, *a one-woman tribute to Pearl S. Buck, produced by Cacciotti. "My mother, who died in 1988, absolutely adored Pearl . . . she read all of her books . . . so I feel as if her hand is very much over us," she said, after the play opened in Chicago.*

But it is TV—where Rhoda continues to live in late-night syndication—where she has had the most visibility. "People always apologize when they ask about Rhoda . . . as if I must get tired of hearing it," Harper said. "But playing that character was a huge gift."

She and Cacciotti live in New York, with their fourteen-year-old daughter, Cristina.

68

• • •

When it comes to thoughts on aging, I'd like to be like Pearl Buck, who said: "It would never occur to me *not* to tell my age, since every year is an added honor."

That reflects the Chinese idea that aging enhances a human being like the patina on a fine antique. But, let's face it, unfortunately that's not what's valued here in the West.

This preoccupation [with outward appearance] is a barrier to expressing ourselves as human beings. It takes tremendous amounts of time, energy, and effort to keep working on the exterior. Our society tends to value you as a commodity with a shelf life, like a tomato.

So, this fuels the race to implants and surgery. I understand the impulse of trying to stave off age and I'm certainly not above it—I dye my hair—but I hope it changes before my daughter turns fifty.

[In a moment of Rhoda-like candor, Harper insisted that I scrutinize her face for any telltale tucks.]

When I was younger, my dream was to be a ballerina—a lot of us got hooked on *The Red Shoes*. But the thought of putting on toe shoes now . . . I can just feel the blisters. Today, I'm just thrilled to be sitting in the audience. Life definitely gets better—and as your history gets longer, you only get more interesting. Ruth Gordon, who once played my mother in a movie called *Don't Go to Sleep,* said that we all have a choice whether to get old or to get older. She chose to get older . . . I think that's great advice: to embrace the inevitable.

It also helps to have something that gives your life purpose and meaning. I'm very involved with The Hunger Project—an organization which has as its purpose the sustainable end of world hunger—and Results, a citizen-action group to eliminate poverty.

69

"Life definitely gets better— and as your history gets longer, you only get more interesting."

The commitment to make a contribution came from my mother. All her life, first as a teacher, then a nurse, and certainly as a parent, she was serving others. Although I found show business irresistible, I have always tried to strike a balance by finding service in my life wherever I could.

So roll up your sleeves and do something—untold joy comes from such action. Don't go to a singles' bar, go to a soup kitchen. Not only does it get you out of yourself—which automatically keeps you young—but you'll meet some of the most wonderful people on both sides of the serving table.

LAUREN HUTTON

70

By the time most models pass thirty-five, they go into retirement. Lauren Hutton, on the other hand, must hold the record for the longest modeling career in history.

When she turned fifty, there were no black balloons and dead flowers. She was featured in a Revlon ad with the seductive copy: "This is our prime time. Let's make the most of it."

A native of Tampa, Florida, Hutton came to New York while still in her teens. Her gap-toothed smile and asymmetrical good looks were discovered by modeling czarina Eileen Ford. For the next three decades, she appeared on the cover of just about every publication except Popular Mechanics.

She has appeared in numerous films, including American Gigolo, Once Bitten, *and* My Father, the Hero. *TV credits include her own talk show and a CBS series,* Central Park West.

Never married, Hutton lives in New York.

• • •

© Laspata/Decabo Studio

"The American woman of my generation

We really are an extraordinary generation. We were the first generation to have rock and roll, birth control, and jobs. We fought like hell to forge our own identity, so maybe that's why I have always been proud of my age.

The American woman of my generation who had the foresight to take care of herself is in an enviable position. She is like the durian, a fruit from Indonesia and the only aphrodisiac I've ever run into. It isn't good until it's absolutely ripe.

My advice is to be a woman instead of a girl. When you hear older women talk about World War II, it was with a certain fondness, as if they missed the war. It was the first time many had their own apartments, their own jobs, when they could even sleep with someone else. They owned their sexuality, they started knowing life outside. Then, the 1950s came and it was all over. Women were shown vacuuming in pearls and heels and housework was made to look glamorous. Why? Because they needed the jobs back for the boys . . . and then it wasn't until the 1960s that women started feeling empowered again. We now know that money is freedom.

The pressure to look young is nothing new. When I was twenty-two, Eileen Ford told me I needed to look seventeen. It all made sense at one time because women literally needed to get a man or perish because they had no way of supporting themselves. But it makes no sense today.

I went through a real bottoming out at around age forty-six and forty-seven. I had just ended a long relationship—one that I had for more than twenty years. I didn't have kids, I no longer loved my work, and I was feeling generally miserable. What made it worse was that I was supposed to be so glamorous. I realized there was

who had the foresight to take care of herself is in an enviable position."

nothing I liked about my life at all. So I went into therapy—which I think is good advice for midlife. You face unresolved issues of your childhood and if you don't, all that pain shows on your face and makes you old—along with lack of sleep.

After that, I just went into another direction, one that addressed age in a whole other way. When I did the Barney ads (which celebrated lovely faces adorned with well-earned wrinkles), women were coming up to me on the street thanking me for it. They were hungry for some honor and respect, especially after all these adolescent models. It is so foolish . . . we're the ones with the money, not fifteen-year-old girls.

So just plow ahead. When breeding shuts down, I think brains get much better, much sharper. Why? Because it's nature's way of compensating—and nature doesn't make mistakes.

ERICA JONG

MAY 26, 1942
WRITER

Erica Jong was barely thirty when she made the best-seller list with her provocative Fear of Flying, *in 1973.*

The daughter of a songwriter-turned-importer and an artist, Jong grew up in New York's Upper West Side and majored in English literature at Barnard College. While she had always been somewhat of an overachiever, nothing prepared her for the tidal wave of early fame. The lusty novel sold a staggering 12.5 million copies in twenty-seven languages.

"What saved me was my sense of humor and the fact that I had a good literary education," she said. "I took as my model the European writers who go on rather than the Americans who burn out and self-destruct."

While Fear *was followed by five books of poetry and seven novels, a children's book and three works of nonfiction, none has matched her earlier success. Most notable among them was* The Devil at Large, *her first full-length work of nonfiction. The 1993*

73

book is a tribute to her inspiration and mentor, Henry Miller, whose Tropic of Cancer *had been banned in the United States for almost three decades. "I had gone from being a young poet to the Queen of Smut. He had been through the same thing, and his understanding kept me going."*

She faced her own midlife crisis in 1994 with a refreshingly candid autobiography, Fear of Fifty. *She lives in New York with her teenage daughter, her husband, and various pets.*

• • •

74

What I find amazing is this need to give something back. I'm starting the Erica Mann Jong Writing Fund at Barnard College, which will provide stipends for young women who teach writing to their peers. I think it's very normal at this stage in life to see how you can nurture the next generation, but I was surprised that the need was so strong . . . it has become almost an obsession with me. Without a doubt, it is the most interesting aspect of getting older. I love the idea of encouraging younger people. It's a new role that you grow into—you become the teacher.

Of course, you also think about your own children. My daughter is leaving for college soon, so I'm very aware about how the cycle gets repeated; how you detach from your own narcissism and begin to see the grand plan of the human race.

Anyone who has had kids knows how hard it is to raise them, but I don't think any generation has faced the problems we have: that switching gears,

"I love the idea of encouraging younger people. It's a new role that you grow into—you become the teacher."

going from one kind of focus to another, from the school play to writing your novel. It is so difficult to do, that a lot of young women don't want to try . . . but a great deal of enrichment comes from switching gears. Children give you a way of marking life, which I find very healing. Writing is one way to contribute; raising children who are thinking and compassionate is another way.

You can accept aging, you can fight it, but you can't reverse it. No matter what you do, youth is not retrievable—and I say that as someone who takes tons of vitamins and works out four times a week. I wouldn't go back to my twenties now for the world—perhaps if I could be twenty-five and know what I do now, but not with the turmoil I felt then.

"In the ten years I've been reading the death notices, I have yet to encounter the praise: 'She maintained her ideal weight.'"

—MARY KAY BLAKELY, author

Living Fit magazine

"Mistakes are part of the dues we pay for a full life."

—SOPHIA LOREN, actress

Great quotes from Great Women

NAOMI JUDD

JANUARY 11, 1946
SINGER

© Lesley Bohm

78

For eight years, Naomi and daughter Wynonna were country superstars, selling fifteen million albums and racking up Grammys with a vengeance.

Then, their lives were shattered in 1990, when Naomi was diagnosed with chronic active hepatitis C and given only a few years to live. After an emotional farewell tour, Naomi left Wynonna to a solo career, quit the road, and went into isolation on her farm in Peaceful Valley, outside Nashville, Tennessee.

"All of a sudden there was no creative challenge . . . no camaraderie, no reason to even get dressed," she said. "I had panic attacks and went into a depression. My therapist told me, 'I've had people lose their career and had people go through life-threatening illnesses or separation from family, but I never had anyone who was going through it all at once.'"

"Once you start to question your life you get to a higher level of awareness.

But even before life took this latest turn, the Judd saga sounds like every country-song cliché: A daughter of a gas station manager struggles through teen pregnancy ("I gave birth to Wynonna on high school graduation night"), death of her younger brother, domestic abuse, raises her two daughters alone while working menial jobs and living on welfare, Mom and daughter discover harmony—more musical than personal—win an RCA contract, and go on to fame and fortune.

Her isolation yielded the best-selling book about her life, Love Can Build a Bridge, *in 1993, which, in turn, inspired a four-hour miniseries. Naomi kept an eye on the filming as co-executive producer. Both daughters Wynonna and Ashley* (Heat, A Time to Kill) *live on farms adjoining their mother's.*

Since retiring from the stage, Naomi has been telling her story on the lecture circuit and opened a restaurant in Nashville. (Her hepatitis is now in remission.)

79

* * *

What I've learned is that control is an illusion and security is a myth. The only thing you have control over is your choices. The only real security comes from knowing that the deepest source of your identity is God.

The point was mercilessly driven home when I got sick. All the things I thought were security—a number one record or winning a Grammy—meant nothing.

Change is the true nature of this world. It's like getting older. There's nothing you can do about it, so you need to go with the flow. I encourage women to question everything in their lives. Why are

It's like turning a light on—voilà—you see you have choices and choices are sacred."

you in this marriage? Why are you in this job? Why is this the status of your relationship with your kid? Once you start to question your life you get to a higher level of awareness. It's like turning a light on—voilà—you see you have choices and choices are sacred. If there is something you cannot change, then change the way you react to it. I used to think that I could do that for people—you know, if I saw a woman on a bus with a black eye, I'd want to go home with her and help her pack—but I realize you can't do it for anyone else. We've all got to do it for ourselves.

Above all, I've learned that peace of mind is the goal. I've been in trailers and penthouses and everyone wants the same thing—and that's peace of mind.

I was in an airport recently and this emaciated man walks up to me with tears in his eyes and says, "Naomi, I'm going home to tell my family I have AIDS. What can you tell me?" I took his hands in mine and said, "Brother, all I can tell you is peace of mind is the goal." Peace isn't the absence of the problem, it's the ability to deal with it. I wanted him to know that there may not be a cure, but there can always be healing—no matter what the prognosis—that this is still within our reach. And you know what? He got it.

When you're in a situation like that with another human being . . . those are the tens on the emotional Richter scale. Very few people get to hear their name called at the Grammys or run out onstage to twenty thousand people at Madison Square Garden, but everyone can reach out to someone else. We're all in this together and we all need each other. We can all be healers.

AUGUST 17, 1944
AUTHOR AND ACTRESS

ELAINE KAGAN

The critical accolades won by her debut novel, The Girls, *established Elaine Kagan as a talent to watch. The fact that she was published for the first time at age fifty made it even sweeter.*

This is really Chapter 2 for Kagan, who already had a thriving acting career, with credits such as Goodfellas *and* Coming to America *on her résumé. But family responsibilities caused her to shift her energies from acting to writing. The result? A page-turner that chronicled the journey of six Midwestern childhood friends reunited at the funeral of one of their husbands.* Mirabella *called it "a hot, sweet, sexy, funny-so-you-cry, right-on look at the way women live their lives."*

In 1996, she followed it with Blue Heaven, *an affecting portrait of a woman trying to cope with an aging parent and a teenage daughter—events plucked, not incidentally, from her own life.*

"I feel very good because what I'm doing now is for me. That is undoubtedly the best part of getting older."

fifty on fifty

• • •

I am living proof that you can change yourself. In fact, a friend pointed out that I seem to have a need to reinvent myself every ten years. I got married in my thirties, became an actress in my forties, and was published at fifty, so I am eager to see what is going to happen at sixty.

I feel very good because what I'm doing now is for me. That is undoubtedly the best part of getting older.

When I was younger, I never felt smart enough. I never thought I was qualified to write. Writers went to places like Yale. I didn't go to college, I was a secretary. Some of this fear is just a holdover from the 1950s—when we were supposed to get an "MRS." degree. We were protected from balancing a checkbook, changing a lightbulb . . . we weren't expected to be anything, do anything, not have our own lives, just be a part of him.

I started writing when my daughter was in kindergarten, just little observations, then the book. I didn't tell anyone I was writing a book because I knew they wouldn't take me seriously. I was married to a film director [Jeremy Kagan] . . . he was the star, I was in the background. The book came out and my nineteen-year marriage ended. It was the best and worst of times—joy and sadness. You spend the better part of your life married and then you're not married anymore—it's lonely and it's frightening. What you realize eventually is that it's better to be alone than to be unhappy in a lonely marriage.

I've learned that life just keeps changing and you have to keep going. It's hard, it's scary, but it's worth it. I'd rather be sobbing at the side of the road than not feeling anything. That much I know.

DONNA KARAN

"That I'm a woman makes me want to nurture others, fulfill needs, and solve problems. How can I make life easier? How can dressing be simplified so we can get on with our lives? How to add comfort and luxury? What will accentuate the positive and delete the negative?"

83

No wonder Donna Karan New York seems to understand the lives of 1990s women so well. Whether it's designing jeans for people who actually have hips or swathing us in luxe fabrics, Karan has an uncanny knack for knowing what we need.

Born Donna Ivy Faske on Long Island in New York, Karan can't remember a time when she wasn't interested in fashion. When she was three, her father died in a car accident and her mother went to work. It was a lonely time—everyone else had a milk-and-cookie mom—but it also fostered a strong streak of independence and flexibility.

Despite being a lackluster student, she was accepted at Parsons School of Design. In addition to talent, Karan also had moxie, applying to Anne Klein for a summer job, after just two years at Parsons. Eventually, Karan became Klein's successor after her death in 1974, just three days after the birth of Karan's daughter. The new chief designer was just twenty-six years old.

The following year, Karan and her longtime friend Louis Dell'Olio designed the collection together, taking the Anne Klein label to the top of the market until 1984, when she went into business for herself with husband Stephan Weiss.

Since then, the company has grown at a dizzying pace—with lines ranging from menswear to makeup—and went public in 1996. Karan has been saluted by her peers with numerous honors, including three Coty Awards. A more significant achievement, however, may be that she is one of the highest-paid executives in corporate America.

Between them, she and Weiss have three children and three grandchildren. They live in New York

84

· · ·

The best part of getting older is that you know yourself better. Who you are, what feels right, what doesn't. You've made the mistakes, you don't have to go through them again. You know where you're going, which direction to take. You trust yourself.

In my mind, I'm always eighteen, but I do think as you get older, you're more in touch with yourself and more comfortable within.

"You can't let your mind get old.

You can't let your mind get old. You always have to be open, always ready to take on new challenges.

Change keeps you young. I'm forever challenging the artist within. Pushing myself out of the comfort zone and venturing into the unknown, the unfamiliar.

Professionally, I'm always looking for what doesn't exist. What isn't out there. What I can't find. If I can't find something new to say or I can't say it better, then I won't say it. That's how DKNY started. I needed a pair of sexy jeans. Menswear? I wanted to dress my husband. Everything I do is highly personal. You have to stay true to your own vision.

More and more, I realize that my success is directly tied into being a woman. Being a mother is the most creative thing you can do. I view my company as a family. The nurturer in me makes me want to bring out the best in others. To reward when things go right, to comfort when they don't. These are strong essential qualities in a leader. The more we access our femininity, the more we realize our unique strength.

The older I get the more I appreciate how profound my parents' influence was. Both of them had the best sense of personal style and always dressed impeccably. You could say I was born into fashion. It was everywhere, starting at the dinner table. My father was a custom tailor, my mother a showroom model. Even my stepfather was in the fashion business. Does this mean I wanted to be a designer? Far from it. All I wanted was to dance like Martha Graham and sing like Barbra Streisand. But ultimately, you have to build on your own talent and do what you do best.

85

You always have to be open, always ready to take on new challenges."

DIANE KEATON

At age fifty-one—twenty years after she won an Oscar as Woody Allen's flustered, WASPy girlfriend Annie Hall—Diane Keaton still exudes a trace of self-deprecating vulnerability.

86

In her illustrious career—which includes such landmark films as The Godfather *trilogy,* Looking for Mr. Goodbar, *and* Reds—Annie Hall *was indeed the most comfortable fit.*

© Brigitte Lacombe

More of a stretch is Marvin's Room, *in which she plays the role of Bessie, the responsible older sister of a dysfunctional clan, which earned her an Academy Award nomination.*

It is a far cry from her own experiences growing up in Santa Ana, California, the oldest of four children of Jack and Dorothy Hall (yes, that really is her last name). Her late father was a civil engineer and her mother won a handful of pageants— including Mrs. Los Angeles—for her ability to bake and clean.

While the domestic point was lost on young Diane, the perform- ing aspect was not. From an early age she showed an affinity for the spotlight—singing in the Methodist church choir and appearing in school musicals and community theater.

After high school, she briefly attended college before going to New York, where she won a minor part in the rock musical Hair. *Several months later, she was the female lead. She was also one of the few cast members who didn't take off her clothes for the final num- ber, despite the fact that it would mean an extra $50 in her paycheck.*

"Standing naked in the dark, getting cold . . . it was just some- thing I didn't want to do."

That role led to Play It Again, Sam, *the first of five films she did with Woody Allen. It also led to the part of Kay, the wife of Mafia don Michael Corleone, considered one of the classics of American cinema. She was all of twenty-three years old. "I felt enormously lucky. To this day, I don't know why I got the part."*

*She worked under some of the best people in the business: direc- tors Allen, Francis Ford Coppola, and Warren Beatty (*Reds) *and cin- ematographer Gordon Willis (*The Godfather *and Woody Allen films). These experts served as an informal film school faculty, and in 1987 she tried her own hand at directing—first, with a droll docu- mentary called* Heaven, *followed by* Unstrung Heroes.

In 1996, she moved back in front of the camera with the box-office bonanza First Wives Club, *as one of three women "of a certain age" who are dumped by their powerful husbands for*

87

"As you get older, the physical deterioration is offset by a larger worldview and a deeper sense of gratitude."

sweet young things. In real life, she lives with her adopted daughter, Dexter, in Los Angeles.

* * *

Plastic surgery is certainly a big topic for all of us girls out there over forty, isn't it? But I have no interest in going under the knife. You're not younger . . . it doesn't fool anyone, so what's the point?

You have so many options taken away from you. You can't be an authentic sixty-year-old character and, at the same time, play an ingenue. I don't believe it for a minute and I don't think the audience does, either. Now, watch me . . . next month, I'll have a facelift and go around with that mask look. But really, the women I admire are the ones who don't do it, like Jessica Tandy.

As you get older, the physical deterioration is offset by a larger worldview and a deeper sense of gratitude.

I've been very privileged—to have met so many different people, to have been exposed to so many different points of view, I feel enormously lucky. There was a time where I hoped that I'd be in a situation—with a husband and a family . . . and that isn't where my life and choices took me. But I don't see it as sad. No one gets everything.

SUZY KELLETT

© Terry Vitacco

Look up "resilient" in the dictionary and you're sure to find a picture of Suzy Kellett.

As a single working mother of quadruplets, Kellett certainly knows how to adapt. After receiving degrees from the University of Denver and Washington State University, she and her husband moved to Idaho, where she was a teacher to rural and migrant children. In 1975, her own four children were born. But when her husband walked out when the quadruplets were ten months old, she moved back home to Chicago.

With the help of her parents and other family members, Kellett was able to "safety-pin" together this house of cards. She landed an entry-level receptionist job at People *magazine, where she moved up the editing ranks, before jumping to* Time *magazine, where she was promoted to Midwest photo editor. Her ability to raise her kids alone gave her the confidence to weather any setback.*

In 1981, she was hired as deputy director of the Illinois Film Office, a job that meant longer hours but more flexibility. Two years

89

later, she became managing director. During her fifteen-year tenure, she attracted a long list of box-office hits to Chicago, including Risky Business, Home Alone, Ordinary People, *and* The Fugitive.

In 1996, she took over the Washington State Film Office—and all four of her children are in college.

• • •

Don't be afraid to throw yourself out of the nest. In 1996, after fifteen years in Illinois, I moved to Seattle because I felt the need for a life change. Truman Capote said, "Life is a play with a bad third act," and I thought, "Not if I can help it." My kids were in college, I had the time, and I've always loved the West, so I did it.

When I made the decision, I could feel this weight falling off my shoulders—it felt so right. I never had any doubts about this, even though it meant leaving family and lots of good friends. I had taken the previous year off, so I spent a lot of time being by myself doing what I wanted to do, which perfectly positioned me to make this move.

I knew there could be times when things would be out of control. When the quads were younger, I had months where I had the sickest kids in the world—times four. You think, "This is just not worth it," but you get through it. Ultimately, we make our choices and I chose to have the quads and my husband chose to walk. Anyways, I gave this move my best shot. I told myself that I was resourceful and had enough experience and that if anything happened, I would find something else . . .

Turning fifty was not a warmly anticipated birthday. Part of that can be chalked up to being single, the other part is that I thought

"The truth is that I really like the ease with which I move through the world right now.

that at the gong of fifty, I would have limited time. But I don't feel that way anymore.

I believe that if you can dream it, you can have it. Most things aren't terminally serious and I view life with a lot more amusement than I did in the past. A sense of humor goes along with good health.

Because this country is very unforgiving about aging, doing it well—with wit, wisdom, grace—is extremely difficult. The truth is that I really like the ease with which I move through the world right now. But I wouldn't mind being cute just one more time . . .

It would be nice to grow old with someone. In your twenties, people get married for passion, in your thirties, it's for children, in your forties, it's for money and prestige. But in your fifties, you want someone who would go through chemotherapy with you. So that's what I'd like to find—someone who would love me without my hair.

91

But I wouldn't mind being cute just one more time . . ."

KAY
KOPLOVITZ

APRIL 11, 1945
CABLE TV PIONEER

92

No one can accuse Kay Koplovitz, chairman and chief executive officer of USA Network, of not thinking big.

In 1977, when she founded TV's first advertiser-supported basic cable network, there wasn't much of a market out there. Now, USA is considered the fifth network behind NBC, ABC, CBS, and Fox, leading all other cable networks in subscribers and revenues since 1990.

What's propelled USA—and Koplovitz—is cable's growth (it's now available in 75 percent of all American homes). She started USA as an all-sports network, negotiating the first national cable rights to major-league baseball, the NBA, and the NHL, before shifting to a general entertainment format. Now, she's channeling her efforts into developing more original programming.

Ask colleagues about Koplovitz and they're sure to mention her insatiable curiosity. Her interest in cable was piqued some thirty years ago, when she was a premed student and heard a talk on satel-

© Emmett Martin

lite transmission. "The idea of completely eliminating borders in communication was so intriguing that I changed my major."

A native of Milwaukee, Koplovitz is a graduate of the University of Wisconsin and also holds a master's degree in communications from Michigan State University. She and her husband, Bill, live in New York City.

• • •

It became apparent to me by the early 1970s that it would be difficult to achieve my goals in traditional TV. As a first-time producer, I'd sit in meetings and notice there were no other female faces. It was pretty clear that they didn't look at me as the future president of NBC.

"It's important to have a formal or informal group of people whom you admire and can learn from because it's just too painful to learn it all yourself."

93

So what do you do? You go somewhere else. I went to a place where I could have a hand in shaping and get the experience I needed and where I could make my mark. That was satellite and cable.

People like to make TV out to be unique, but I'm not so sure there are a lot of differences from other industries . . . where control is in the hands of men and change comes slowly. At one point, women who sat on boards were wealthy widows. Today, women are asked to serve because of their business experience.

The most important wisdom I can offer is to never let others define your horizons. Identify what success means to you and then keep your eye on that prize. Do not be distracted; know that there is almost an environmental predisposition for not selecting women to head companies. But if this is your goal, then you have to be singular in your desire to get there, to aspire to that level.

Also, seek out mentors. It helps to have the wisdom of someone else who navigated the waters. No matter how self-reliant you are, there are times in everyone's career where you will need someone to go to bat for you. It's important to have a formal or informal group of people whom you admire and can learn from because it's just too painful to learn it all yourself.

The perception of where vitality resides is changing; it's less age-based than ever before. All of us who build companies look to youth to provide the next generation of leadership. But career women in midlife are sought after because they were trailblazers—and that's a highly prized attribute.

The age limits are constantly being pushed upward because people are working longer. If you want to retire at fifty and start something new, you can do it and have another twenty-five years left. One of the reasons I do what I do is because I was fascinated with satellite technology. I love the process of discovery. Whether it's business, science, or medicine, as long as you can cut new roads, you're going to be excited by your work.

To me, the rewards are in challenging your mind and your capabilities, whether you succeed or fail—and, believe me, we do both.

PATTI LaBELLE

MAY 24, 1944
SINGER

© Albert Sanchez/MCA Records

Patti LaBelle has been a member of "girl groups" since the 1960s, when she was just a teen living in a gritty neighborhood in South Philadelphia. In the 1980s she dominated the music scene by deftly combining spectacle and the soul sound. In between, Patti has earned numerous awards and a reputation as one of America's most flamboyant and enduring show business divas.

It has been a bumpy ride, both personally and professionally. Singing provided LaBelle with a way to overcome a paralyzing case of shyness, and her group—the Ordettes—would eventually go on to become Patti LaBelle and the Bluebelles. In 1962 she took off with her first multimillion-seller, "I Sold My Heart to the Junkman."

But the group pulled in different directions and eventually dis-

solved in 1976. Despite her fears, she launched a solo career—racking up hits like "Over the Rainbow," "Lady Marmalade," and "Somebody Loves You"—and broadened her appeal by appearing on Broadway and in the movie A Soldier's Story. *At the same time, she kept on recording, capturing a 1992 Grammy for Best Female Vocalist.*

Out of the spotlight, though, her life was marred by tragedy. Although she enjoyed a solid marriage (to Armstead Edwards, her manager) and motherhood, she lost her own mother to diabetes and her father to Alzheimer's disease. All three of her sisters—along with her best friend—succumbed to cancer while still in their early forties. The deaths took their toll, leaving LaBelle with the persistent fear that she would never live to see her fiftieth birthday.

96

●   ●   ●

I thought I had as much a chance reaching fifty as I did one hundred fifty. All my life, death has been in my face, taking what was mine . . . what I needed most and loved best.

I can't even describe the terror as my birthday approached . . . I wouldn't even allow myself to hope [that I'd be the only one of four daughters] to survive. The only way for me to cope was to throw myself into my work like a madwoman—concerts, clubs, running all over the country. But as long as I kept moving, I felt like I could run away from everything.

When I finally reached fifty, I could finally let go of that fear. It was one of the most amazing experiences of my life . . . My party was held at the House of Blues [in Los Angeles], and I felt like an absolute queen. It was so freeing—like I had finally been released—

"Take care of friendships, hold people you love close to you,

and since then I'm so peaceful. Everything is better . . . I use time better, I love better, I live better. I had no idea how precious time was until I lost my sisters—they all died within five years . . . and I could have used that time better. When I was younger I took people for granted, and that is a regret I'll always have.

But maybe others will learn from my mistakes. Since I went on this book tour [for *Don't Block the Blessings*], so many people have come up to me and said "I had a falling out with my mother" or "I haven't spoken to my sister in years, but I'm going to call her tonight." I couldn't be there for my sister [Jacqueline]—when I did, they had already pulled the sheet over her—but maybe my story will mean someone will be there for their sister.

Here's what I know: I'm a better person at fifty than I was at forty-eight . . . and better at fifty-two than I was at fifty. I'm calmer, easier to live with. All this stuff is in my soul forever.

Just don't get lazy. Work at your relationships all the time. Take care of friendships, hold people you love close to you, take advantage of birthdays to celebrate fiercely. It's the worrying—not the years themselves—that will make you less of a woman.

97

take advantage of birthdays to celebrate fiercely."

ELLEN LEVINE

© Timothy White

In 1994, Ellen Levine made publishing history when she became the first woman to be named editor-in-chief of Good Housekeeping *since the magazine was founded in 1885.*

But even before her appointment to the top post of Hearst's flagship publication, she had established a reputation for journalistic excellence. She had served as editor-in-chief at Redbook *and* Woman's Day, *leaving both stronger—editorially and financially—than when she had arrived.*

After graduating from Wellesley College, she went to work as a reporter at The Record *in Hackensack, New Jersey, then moved on to* Cosmopolitan, *where she served as senior editor. In addition, she has written several books that reflect the life cycle, from* Planning Your Wedding *to* Rooms That Grow with Your Child.

Throughout her career, she has received numerous honors. In 1986, the American Society of Journalists and Authors presented her with an award for courage in the pursuit of truth, the result of her work as a member of the U.S. Attorney General's Commission on Pornography.

Levine served as president of the American Society of Magazine Editors (ASME) and is currently on the boards of several organizations, including the National Alliance of Breast Cancer Organizations and Covenant House. She resides with her husband, Richard, a physician, in New York. They have two sons.

· · ·

One of the worst things anyone can do is not take a vacation. You need to just go somewhere and wash your brain out. I find that if you let yourself truly rest, your enthusiasm will grow. It works the same way as pruning back a plant.

I get away as far as I can to a place with no phones and no newsstands because I have an addiction to both. I see ideas wherever I go. I was the editor of my newspaper in the sixth grade and in high school, so I'm very fortunate that what turned me on at sixteen is what turns me on today.

But that doesn't mean I don't have a daily fear of failing. I'm not sure you ever get over that feeling, where you wake up each day, telling yourself, "I've got to try harder." I have certain mantras for those times, like "I've done this before" or "I'll get through this," or I'll conjure up images of making my goal. But I do tend to compete against myself instead of against others.

One thing I don't understand is retirement. What is this? So you can do all the things you've wanted to do? You should be doing that throughout your life. Also, if you use your brain, I figure, it will keep working. It's my way of defying Alzheimer's.

> "I find that if you let yourself truly rest, your enthusiasm will grow. It works the same way as pruning back a plant."

I have always worked . . . even when my kids were young. Honestly, looking back, I don't feel like I missed out on anything.

My role model was Miriam Petrie, my first boss at *The Record*. She was a widow, raising three kids, and she was head of the women's page. She raised these kids without a lot of money and never questioned it. She also supported women and believed I could do anything.

I never thought about other careers. I applied to Dow Jones, but they didn't take women. I was never angry about it, which shows you how dopey I was. But at the time, running a company or working on Wall Street were never on my radar screen.

My advice to other women is not to be so anxious to get ahead. When we started, the concept of a career path didn't exist. Opportunities opened up because you created them. Some people get lucky breaks and just fall into things, but mostly they come because you worked hard and played fair. Don't be too hungry, too aggressive—if you burn a lot of people along the way, it catches up with you.

Also, know when to ignore things. I used to feel that I had to deal with absolutely everything, particularly with my staff. My husband told me, "If I ran into the operating room every time something went wrong, I'd be operating twice as much as necessary." Now I know that some things heal themselves.

DONNA LOPIANO

© Beth Green Studios

Donna Lopiano's consciousness was raised in the sixth grade, when she was denied a spot on the local Little League team, despite having the fastest arm in Stamford, Connecticut. She wasn't just good for a girl. She was good period. Up until that moment, Lopiano believed with every ounce of her being that she could be the next Mickey Mantle.

The outside world, however, saw it differently. So when Lopiano felt the sting of rejection that summer of 1957, she channeled her energy into softball instead, ultimately playing on six national championship teams and earning a place in the National Softball Hall of Fame.

After graduating with a Ph.D. in physical education in 1974, she became director of women's athletics at the University of Texas. Title IX—the federal legislation that made gender discrimination illegal—had just become law and Lopiano was about as welcome as *a rash. But she stood up to Darrell Royal, UT's legendary football coach, beefing up her budget by more than $3 million and turning the Lady Longhorns into what* Sports Illustrated *called "the gemstone of all collegiate programs, male or female."*

Today, as head of the Women's Sports Foundation, Lopiano continues to be one of the country's most articulate champions of equal opportunity in sports. She is single and lives in New York.

. . .

No question being told no had defined me. Here, I had trained to be a major-leaguer—and that path goes through Little League. That's why I'm in the business I'm in. No child—male or female—should ever be told they can't pursue a dream.

One of the things that sport teaches you is that this is all a game. You lose one, but you play again tomorrow. You're going to make mistakes, but the idea is not to make the same mistake twice. Keep going, keep reconfiguring . . . it's not a straight line.

Don't be afraid to show a little chutzpah. It's what I needed to exist in the same world as Texas football. And there is no power greater than persistence. If you just stay with it long enough, one of three things will happen: Either you wear down your opponent, they retire, or they die. Eventually, you're the only one left standing.

Yes, at times it was hard taking on the football coach at Texas, the NCAA (which she took to court in an antitrust suit in 1981), but things change and the day will come when the time is right—but one thing is certain: It can't be right if you're not there.

In my current position, the landscape is broader. It reaches into corporate America and the U.S. Olympic Committee, TV and adver-

"You're going to make mistakes, but the idea is not to make the same mistake twice.

tising, collegiate and high school sports. We're bursting myths—about how good women can be, about whether fans will come to watch women play, and about how Americans are ready to embrace the female athlete. It's about having the power to impact the way people think.

Sure, there were times I doubted whether I could get the job done. It's very easy to let things get you down—especially in a world that was previously all-male. Whenever I hit one of these stone walls, I figure that there's got to be a way around this. It helps to depersonalize the obstacle, as if it were just another piece on the chess board.

What gets me excited is that in 1972, one in twenty-seven girls participated in sports; now it's one in three. There's a critical mass of women thirty-five and under who now identify more with their physical self. And that's really something. It's rather nice to sit back and watch this happen because you never thought you would.

I would not redo anything because you couldn't just redo the good things and I'm not willing to go through the bad things all over again. But this much I know: If you can't look back and say it was great fun, then it wasn't worth it.

Keep going, keep reconfiguring . . . it's not a straight line."

"Expect trouble as an inevitable part of life and repeat to yourself the most comforting words of all, this, too, shall pass."

—ANN LANDERS, syndicated columnist

SUSAN LOVE

FEBRUARY 9, 1948
SURGEON AND AUTHOR

If you are a woman with breast cancer, you couldn't ask for a more rock-solid ally than Dr. Susan Love.

Since she entered the health profession more than twenty years ago, Love's dedication to women's health issues—particularly breast cancer—has reshaped the medical establishment's treatment of women.

105

As the only woman in the operating room at the Revlon/UCLA Medical Center in Los Angeles, Love gave patients a voice when they needed it most. She questioned the conventional treatment of radical mastectomies, chemotherapy, and radiation (calling it "slash, poison, and burn") and pioneered lumpectomies, a less invasive procedure. In 1991, she co-founded the National Breast Cancer Coalition, an umbrella organization for advocacy groups.

Love is critical of doctors for jumping on the medical bandwagon—silicone implants and IUDs, for example—without sufficient

© Dana Jones

research. Most of all, she is determined that the 180,000 American women who are diagnosed with breast cancer annually have the facts they need to make informed decisions. So, in 1990, she wrote Dr. Susan Love's Breast Book, *which has become a virtual bible on the subject.*

Said Love: "I don't think about rules very much until they come back to bite me."

The oldest of five, the New Jersey native was turned on to science in junior high by a nun who was her biology teacher. After graduating from Fordham University, she studied medicine at SUNY Brooklyn.

In 1996, at the top of her profession, she left her clinical practice in order to tackle broader issues in women's health. She also finished a book on menopause, raising the same kind of questions on hormone replacement therapy that she did for breast cancer.

She lives in Los Angeles with her partner and fellow surgeon, Dr. Helen Cooksey, and her nine-year-old daughter.

* * *

I had been doing direct patient care for almost twenty years . . . and it was getting harder and harder to do it well. There is a degree of burnout when you see women with breast cancer. With each passing year, the difference between you and the patient gets smaller and smaller. After a while, they look like you, they have families and careers like you, and it gets tougher to detach. You either have to put up a wall—which is not my style—or you have to stop. So I stopped.

My short-term goal is to get a master's degree in business at UCLA. It's going to be tough to be a student again—the last time I did this, there were no calculators—but I think it's important to master the language of business, if we're going to figure out a way to deliver quality health care in a managed care environment.

The first wave of managed care was to compete on cost, but now we're going to see the second wave—and that will be to compete on quality. Businesspeople didn't know enough about medicine—what to throw out, what to keep—so being "bilingual" will become even more valuable.

"As women, we're lucky because we are reminded in a very physical way that this is midlife, so we can reevaluate what we are and where we're going."

I've always had these grandiose plans to save the world, so my long-term goal is a nonprofit think tank to study women's health issues; to be a "conscience." It was a tough decision [to leave], but it's not like I'm going to go twiddle my thumbs. I'm just taking medicine to another level.

107

I think some of this was triggered by writing about menopause. As women, we're lucky because we are reminded in a very physical way that this is midlife, so we can reevaluate what we are and where we're going.

Many women find that it's a time to shift away from their families and to look outward. For twenty years, we've been there for everybody; it's very healthy to view menopause as a chance to recharge and rebuild.

Doing this kind of work has certainly made me aware of keeping priorities straight; of the need to live as healthy a life as I can, but to still enjoy myself—to me, chocolate is a vegetable. If I've learned anything, it's that you can do all the right things and still have breast cancer . . . and wouldn't it have been a shame to miss dessert or that glass of wine?

TAMMY FAYE BAKKER MESSNER

MARCH 7, 1942
TELEVANGELIST

Long before Tammy Faye and Jim Bakker became a national punch line, they were the brightest stars on Christian television and their theme park, Heritage USA, was the third biggest tourist destination in the country.

Then it all unraveled, starting with allegations of rape by former church secretary Jessica Hahn and ending with Jim Bakker's conviction of defrauding followers of PTL— the ministry the Bakkers founded—of $158 million. (Released from prison in 1996, he no longer communicates with Tammy.)

© George Lange/Villard

Tammy Faye LaValley grew up in northern Minnesota, one of ten children. Her mother's divorce brought shame and ostracism upon the family—especially from their fellow Assemblies of God members. Shy

"I love being fifty—you don't have to prove anything to anyone anymore.

and retiring, it wasn't until she went off to Bible college in Minneapolis and met "that fabulous Bakker boy" that she did much dating.

After a whirlwind courtship, they married at age twenty-one, living on "love offerings" as they they worked their way through the South as traveling pastors. When they hooked up with Pat Robertson—owner of the Christian Broadcasting Network—in the mid-1960s, the Bakkers saw TV as the wave of the future. They came up with the idea of a Johnny Carson–style set—complete with band and sidekick. Seven years later, after a falling-out with Robertson, the duo struck out on their own. The empire grew until its well-publicized demise in 1987.

*Today, Tammy has a new mate, Roe Messner, a developer and former PTL associate who was also convicted of bankruptcy fraud. She also penned a book (*Tammy: Telling It My Way*) and is a spokesman for a wig company. But in 1996, just when things were looking up, she was diagnosed with colon cancer. After surgery, she said, her prognosis is excellent.*

But some scars take longer to heal. In her book, the dedication is to her children, Tammy Sue and Jamie: "I love you my precious children and I am sorry you had to grow up so fast."

* * *

The most important thing I've learned in life is that you think everything is supposed to be fair. Honey, nothing is fair. If kids could learn that at a very young age, they'd be a lot happier.

I have found myself in some very desperate situations, where I just wanted to die. I could have given up, quit eating, locked myself in a room, but it's my attitude that's saved me. I've told myself: "I'm

It absolutely sets a woman free."

not going to let this beat me. I'm going to hold my head up high and make the best of a bad situation." So attitude is the best advice I can give, because all of life is an attitude. There are lot of people who feel sorry for themselves and I know that pity parties will kill you. If you do have one, make it a short one.

I'll tell you what positive attitude can do: After I found out that I had cancer and they took fourteen inches of my colon, I healed three weeks faster than normal. It's right there in Romans 8:28. If you truly believe, you can't help but have the right attitude.

I also believe that you learn to forgive people who have hurt you. It's not something that's easy or automatic, it's a conscious choice . . . just like being angry is a choice. People ask if I think about the past. Of course I do, but I don't dwell on it. It's like that story about the bird. You can't stop a bird from flying over your head, but you don't have to build a nest in your hair, either.

There will always be mean-spirited people, so I've learned to just stay away from them. They have the right to their opinions and I'm not going to try to change their minds. That would be another lesson: Rarely can you change people's minds.

I love being fifty—you don't have to prove anything to anyone anymore. It absolutely sets a woman free. I feel younger, more vibrant . . . I may have less confidence in people, but I have more confidence in God.

CAROL MOSELEY-BRAUN

AUGUST 16, 1947
U.S. SENATOR

courtesy of Carol Moseley-Braun

The first African-American woman elected to the U.S. Senate, Carol Moseley-Braun rode the Chicago patronage system and voter outrage over the Anita Hill hearings to a surprise victory in 1992.

At the time that Moseley-Braun announced her candidacy, the Illinois Democrat was an unknown. Her low-level post as Cook County recorder of deeds hardly provided the kind of power base she would need to launch a campaign—especially against a longtime, popular incumbent, Alan Dixon. But a funny thing happened on the way to the polls.

First, the more Americans watched the televised confirmation hearings of Clarence Thomas—then a nominee for the Supreme

Court—and the way the all-white male senators grilled Anita Hill— a former colleague of Thomas's who accused him of sexual harassment—the angrier they got.

Second, Dixon and another challenger, Al Hofeld, spent their campaigns beating up on each other, allowing Moseley-Braun to sneak in and steal the Democratic primary.

Moseley-Braun went on to win the general election against Richard Williamson, a conservative, thanks to a large number of Republican women who crossed over to send a black woman to the Senate.

The euphoria over her election had barely subsided when a series of scandals erupted: staff complaints about her campaign manager/ boyfriend, an ill-timed vacation to Africa, financial improprieties involving her mother's Medicaid benefits, and meeting with a Nicaraguan dictator. The controversies have caused her public approval ratings to plummet.

Even so, Moseley-Braun has had a few shining moments since arriving in Washington. Most notable: her standoff with Jesse Helms in 1993 over renewing a design patent for the United Daughters of the Confederacy, whose emblem includes the Confederate flag. Calling the flag "an insult" to millions of African-Americans, she vowed to filibuster "until this room freezes over." Actually, it took just three hours for the Senate to reverse itself.

The oldest of four children, Moseley-Braun graduated from the University of Illinois at Chicago in 1969 with a political science degree and the University of Chicago Law School in 1973. Five years later, she won her first bid to the Illinois legislature, where she remained for almost a decade and learned the fine art of consensus-building.

Currently, she is gearing up for what is expected to be a tough 1998 Senate campaign. She is divorced and has a teenage son.

. . .

I've endured a lot and, through it all, you just have to stay focused on who you are and remain grounded. The same strength that carries you through any other endeavor will carry you through in times of crisis.

What works for me is to reach back to my faith [she was raised a Roman Catholic, but describes herself as a born-again Christian]. I don't see how people who don't

"What drives me is the belief that, by my very presence, I can make a contribution."

have it can function. It's where I get the strength to face up to adversity—I draw a lot from the whole notion of suffering and redemption.

What drives me is the belief that, by my very presence, I can make a contribution. The [confrontation] with Jesse Helms is a prime example. It started out as a very bad day. I had already had one argument that equated *Roe v. Wade* with *Plessy v. Ferguson* [the landmark 1896 decision upheld "separate but equal" railway cars]. Then, I had to deal with the Confederate flag and Jesse Helms. But because I am fortunate enough to be in the Senate, I am able to add my voice and that makes a difference. If I were intimidated, then the reason for my being there would be totally diminished.

You pay a price for being out on a limb, for being first. If you could fit my personal philosophy on a T-shirt, it would be the slogan of the Children's Defense Fund: "Dear Lord, please be good to me because the sea is so wide and my boat is so small."

Perhaps because of where I'm at right now in my life, getting older doesn't bother me. I remember turning thirty as being tough, but I'm not worried about fifty. I have too much to accomplish. I have already made history; now I want to make a difference.

113

ANNE MURRAY

JUNE 20, 1945
SINGER

© James O'Mara/O'Mara & Ryan

Anne Murray's career has spanned twenty-nine years and twenty-nine albums— a remarkable accomplishment in the fickle world of pop music.

The Canadian singer has not merely endured—she has flourished, racking up a mountain of honors, including four Grammys, three American Music Awards, and her own star at Hollywood and Vine. She routinely sells out venues, from Carnegie Hall to Las Vegas.

Born in the coal mining town of Springhill, Nova Scotia, Murray grew up as the only girl in a family of five boys. She loved music, but got her degree in physical education "for something to fall back on." After graduation, she auditioned for a TV show. She didn't get the part, but two years later, the host of the show tracked her down and *persuaded her to give it another try. Not only did she get the part, but she also married the host, Bill Langstrongth. Her first big hits were "Snowbird" in 1970 and "Danny's Song" in 1973. Her world-wide album sales are in excess of 25 million. Needless to say, she never taught gym again.*

For Murray, the source of her wisdom came from the death of her longtime mentor and manager, Leonard Rambeau, of cancer in 1995.

* * *

I know the importance of gathering good people around you and to use their talents wisely.

There's a lot to be said for being a good listener, too. I am a great one for taking advice, for being open-minded, for soliciting the opinions of others. I'm a "gleaner" and I think that's been the key to my success—not just in the business, but in life.

There is such value in treating people well, in basic civility. I think that's one of the reasons that people have always been there for me. I'm very proud of the fact that the newest member of my band has been with me for thirteen years. People are always struck with how long we've been together and the great camaraderie we share. In this business, such loyalty is rare, so it's very meaningful. You definitely get it back. Never shut people out, especially if you expect to have a long career. I don't think I ever really did, but I see the importance of it even more clearly now than I did when I was younger.

Leonard was the one person who I felt was indispensable. After he died, I wanted to throw in the towel, but he would not have wanted that to happen, so I've learned how strong I can be; that when a part of you goes, you have to fill in the void and just start over. You push

"We're all more capable than we think we are."

things here and you push things there and hope for the best.

I found that it was not unlike losing a spouse. My mom—who is now in her eighties—knew nothing about business affairs when my dad died. Now, she handles them quite nicely. He [Rambeau] handled the politics of the business and the balance sheets and things I'd rather stay out of. Since he died, I found out that I still don't like it, but I'm not bad at it. Such changes force us to make discoveries about ourselves. We're all more capable than we think we are.

Also, I appreciate my fans. Earlier in my career, I was so caught up with my kids [William and Dawn, now twenty and eighteen, respectively], the house, the road, I didn't have the time to show that appreciation. Now, I can and I don't take it for granted.

I get letters all the time from people who tell me that my music got them through an illness or a death. Early on, I was scared to death of the weight of that responsibility. Now I realize how fortunate I have been to have made a difference. That gives you a reason for being . . . and makes all those years of hard work worthwhile.

K.T. OSLIN

MAY 15, 1942
SINGER AND SONGWRITER

© Mark Seliger

She took Nashville by storm in 1987 with a song called "80's Ladies." Then she proved that she was more than a one-hit wonder with "Do Ya'," which again clinched the number one spot.

But it's been a strange road to stardom for this Arkansas-born and Texas-reared New Yorker. For starters, it didn't happen till she was forty-five, after laboring many years in TV commercials to pay the rent. ("I had a hemorrhoid commercial that had people I knew from third grade calling me up saying, 'Is that you?'")

She finally found a home in country music, exploding onto the scene with 80's Ladies, *which became the highest charting female debut album in country history. In 1988, she had two albums go gold and was the toast of the industry. She won the Country Music Award Female Vocalist of the Year and the CMA Song of the Year— the first ever awarded to a female composer—followed by two Grammys, beating out such established stars as Reba McEntire, Rosanne Cash, and Emmylou Harris.*

The following year, she didn't even rate a nomination.

117

fifty on fifty

In the early 1990s, she released the album Love in a Small Town *and a greatest hits collection (*Songs from an Aging Sex Bomb*), but by 1994, the creative engine had sputtered. She slowly withdrew from the music business and "simply wandered home to garden, paint, visit friends, and build miniatures."*

The hiatus made her realize how much she missed recording. She had already begun researching songs, when she fell ill while mowing her lawn. The next day she underwent quadruple bypass heart surgery. Five months later she was back in the studio, working on My Roots Are Showing, *which many consider her best album yet.*

Never married, Oslin splits her time between New York and Nashville.

* * *

I had heart bypass surgery in 1995. Everybody thinks I came out of this near-death experience and saw angels and light and got this idea for this album [*My Roots Are Showing*]. But it wasn't like that at all. There was no big revelation . . . I never had that fear of dying—if anything, I had no feeling at all. Maybe that was best.

After the fact, I saw the surgery on the Discovery Channel and it was like "Gosh . . . I didn't know they actually stopped the heart." I talked to Larry King and he wanted to know everything the doctors were doing, but I just went into shutdown.

I know that the usual thing that happens when you go through something like this is to say how wonderful life is. But I knew that already. Even before surgery, I did a pretty good job of stopping to smell the roses. But it does have a humbling effect on you. You become more sensitive . . . more aware of other people's plights, which is an advantage for a performer because you can feel the audi-

118

"There's just a lot of mediocrity out there and you must do your best to not contribute to it."

ence. Now, performing live is like marrying everyone in the audience for two hours.

Aging does catch you off guard. Like most people, I thought I'd be freeze-framed at forty. Recently, I was shopping and I looked real schleppy with no makeup on—I caught my reflection in the store window and said, "Mother?" I thought, "Oh, my God . . . when did I start looking just like her?"

When you're young, time creeps by—you're sitting in a classroom and you think three o'clock will never come. But as you age, you're struck with how both the good and the bad go so quickly—and that one is usually right behind the other. When you're young, you think there is one magical age when everything will fall perfectly into place—the perfect mate, the perfect child, the perfect house—right down to the backyard barbecue and the dog. If I've learned anything, it's that it rarely all comes together at one time. You can have success, but it will never be what you envisioned.

I have also learned that there's just a lot of mediocrity out there and you must do your best to not contribute to it. You don't need twenty-five albums, seventeen of them mediocre, two of them great, and one of them phenomenal. You need a phenomenal album and you don't need the rest of them.

Maybe it was the surgery or just that I've been around too long. I just don't want to waste my time anymore. I've discovered that I'm happy being a homebody—in fact, I'd call these "the bathrobe years."

Turning forty, I had a great wingding because I was still a fox, but turning fifty, I was menopausal. When you turn sixty, maybe you get a wingding again—preferably in your bathrobe.

119

LETTY COTTIN POGREBIN

JUNE 9, 1939
WRITER

© Nadine Markova

From feminism to friendship, Letty Cottin Pogrebin has held up a mirror at every critical juncture of her life so we may better examine ours.

Pogrebin is best known as a founder of Ms. *magazine, where she served as an editor for seventeen years. She is the author of eight books, including* How to Make It in a Man's World; Growing Up Free, *a groundbreaking guide to nonsexist child-rearing;* Family Politics, *an analysis of family power relations;* Among Friends, *a lively exploration of friendship; and* Deborah, Golda and Me, *on what it means to be female and Jewish in America. Her most recent literary effort,* Getting Over, Getting Older, *was*

"We can't be young again, but we can be new.

roundly praised for its candor and honesty in confronting the indignities that go with fading youth and in refocusing midlifers on time rather than age.

She has won numerous awards, including an Emmy for her work on the TV special Free to Be . . . You and Me *and Yale University's Poynter Fellowship in Journalism.*

She and her husband, Bert, have three grown children and live in New York City.

* * *

I'm trying to change age obsession into time obsession. When you're aware of time, you use it more mindfully. You live with a consciousness of how precious it is. The people who understand this concept best are those who have had a diagnosis of cancer . . . their priorities fall into place and they don't allow themselves to get mired in trivia. In other words, a true recognition of mortality distills the meaning of life and makes us grateful for every moment.

Another good example is what happens to you on vacation, when you're tuned in to all stimuli—the art and architecture, the food, the faces, even the cobblestones. You notice everything because it's all new. If you're away for one week, it feels like two, but when you return friends say, "Are you back already?" because, for them, time just flew by in a blur of routines, while you slowed it down by savoring it. If you can take the lesson of the vacation experience into your daily life, you can actually succeed at slowing down time.

So I try to do one new thing every day—if it's picking up a book by an unfamiliar author or even sitting in a different chair with my morning coffee, if only to see my house from a fresh perspective to keep the mind alert and alive.

Make a vow to take up three new challenges."

fifty on fifty

The challenge of midlife is to find a balance between the familiar and the new—otherwise you stop growing. The quickest way to age is to disengage, to settle into a well-worn groove. But if you take on a major new challenge every few years—something that asks more of you—you will never stagnate. That can be learning a language, a sport, or correcting a flaw or a fear you've been carrying around for years. You need something to get up for in the morning . . . that's what makes people feel young because it reminds them of childhood, when everything was new.

We can't be young again, but we can be new. Make a vow to take up three new challenges. Mine was to take up a sport, because all my life I had been a wimp—and because I had put on seventeen pounds in three years. I discovered that I really liked walking and now I do three miles a day and even take hiking vacations. This is something I can actually get better at. In fact, I'm stronger at fifty-six than I was at thirty. I am learning Hebrew and I've beaten my blood phobia, something I've been struggling with since I was a kid. These are examples of where time delivered progress. Time has become the conduit for positive change, not just decay. Time has made me stronger and healthier.

I learned that I can't do anything about the length of my life, but I can do something about its width and its depth.

STEFANIE POWERS

NOVEMBER 2, 1945
ACTRESS

courtesy of Stefanie Powers

The fact that Stefanie Powers routinely shuttles between Africa, Paris, and Los Angeles sums up her attitudes on aging.

Best known as the star of the popular series Hart to Hart, *Powers played the role of amateur sleuth Jennifer to Robert Wagner's Jonathan. For five years, the duo brought a wit and style reminiscent of the William Powell/Myrna Loy* Thin Man *movies of the 1930s to 1980s TV.*

In the midst of the run, her longtime companion, William Holden, died. In his memory, she helped establish the William Holden Wildlife Foundation. Using a $250,000 inheritance from his estate and plans the actor drew up himself some fifteen years earlier, Powers and four others created a center to protect endangered

123

species on Holden's 1,200-acre Mount Kenya Game Ranch. (In a cruel twist of fate, Robert Wagner's wife, Natalie Wood, died two weeks after Holden.)

She was born in Hollywood as Stefanie Zofja Federkievicz. Her first love was animals, and she dreamed of a career as a veterinarian or an archaeologist until she landed a few small roles for Columbia Pictures. But she never found her niche in film. Instead, she moved to TV, where her debut was a dreadful 1966 series, The Girl from UNCLE. *Other projects followed, none of them successful. She finally hit the jackpot with* Hart to Hart, *which came along in 1979 and still airs in syndication.*

Most recently, she has toured with the play Love Letters, *but her travels (she speaks French, Polish, Italian, Spanish, Swahili, and Mandarin Chinese) and other projects take priority. In 1993, she married a French businessman, Patrick de la Chenais, who lives in Paris.*

*　*　*　*

There are two quotes that really hit home for me. When Alice Roosevelt Longworth was asked, "To what do you attribute long life?" she answered, "Arrested development." The other is from Auntie Mame: "Life is a banquet and most poor suckers are starving to death."

I know the importance of uncontrollable curiosity. I can't stand having an opportunity and not taking advantage of it. It's the thrill of adventure that keeps me going.

I am surprised when I hear other women say that their choices are diminishing as they get older. To me, there seem to be even more opportunities opening up.

"I know the importance
of uncontrollable curiosity.
I can't stand having
an opportunity and not
taking advantage of it."

Perhaps that's because I'm not one to be intensely focused on myself, which frees me up to enjoy life a lot more. Being self-centered is an invitation to be held hostage to all your fears and insecurities. If I worried about all the things that could go wrong, I'd never leave the house. So I take my causes seriously, but not myself seriously.

I think it's fair to say that age is a nonissue with me. I had a long-term relationship with Bill Holden—who was twenty-six years older than me—and now I'm married to someone who is eight years younger. In addition, I live with my eighty-four-year-old mother, who runs around with a diamond stud in her nose.

Every once in a while I have to remind myself that I'm not twenty years old anymore. I pick up a script and automatically start reading the younger girl's part, when it's really the mother they want me to play. I just keep forgetting.

I do know this: that all the women I admire are the adventurers . . . the indefatigable travelers and Margaret Meads of the world. I once saw an interview on TV with a ninety-year-old woman who stepped off a yak after trekking in Mustang [Nepal]. That's the person I want to be, not the empress dowager with the jewels hanging from her neck.

LYNN REDGRAVE

MARCH 8, 1943
ACTRESS

126

© Catherine Ashmore

The youngest child of an illustrious British theatrical clan that spans four generations, Lynn Redgrave had no desire to join the family business.

In school, the entire sum of her acting consisted of playing a shepherd in a nativity play. But it was only a matter of time until those famous genes would kick in, and, at nineteen, she joined the Royal Court Theatre in London.

Four years later, the 1966 film Georgy Girl *thrust her into stardom. For her portrayal of a warmhearted young woman "who just missed being beautiful," she earned a Golden Globe and New York Film Critics Award, as well as an Academy Award nomination. Not bad for your first movie.*

Subsequent film credits—A Deadly Affair, The Happy Hooker— would follow, but nothing would duplicate her early success.

Other troubles brewed on the horizon: In 1981, she sued Universal Studios, the producer of her TV series House Calls, *for*

"Once you take a stand, you can't say 'never mind' when things get tough . . .

banning her infant daughter from the premises. The case dragged through the courts for fifteen years and exacted a heavy toll, both professionally and personally. Except for Weight Watchers commercials, job offers vanished, and she filed for bankruptcy.

But the dry spell also gave her an opportunity to write Shakespeare for My Father, *a one-woman show about the complex relationship with her late father, Sir Michael Redgrave. While the patriarch was expansive on stage, he was miserly with his emotions at home, which affected Lynn deeply. It pained her to learn that, on the day of her birth, his diary made no mention of the event.*

When Sir Michael died in 1985, she embarked on "a daughter's search for her father's heart." The play ran for nine months on Broadway and captured a Tony nomination.

In 1996, she returned to the screen in the critically acclaimed film Shine. *She lives in California with her producer/husband, John Clark, and their three children.*

•   •   •

Shine was my first film role in six years—it was the most extraordinary fate. Scott Hicks [the director] was in Houston making a documentary, when he saw *Shakespeare for My Father.*

I didn't expect to get anything more than a trip to Australia out of the deal. Who could know that Scott would make such a brilliant film?

It felt wonderful to be back [in film] after so long. There were times when I would get discouraged and want to throw in the towel, but once you take a stand, you can't say "never mind" when things get tough. If you do, you won't be able to look yourself in the mirror. You have to stick to the road.

You have to stick to the road."

I'm not saying that I was blacklisted, but I was punished. If you were a producer, it wasn't too smart to have my name attached to your project . . . jobs that looked like offers always had a way of disappearing.

I was so naive when I started this [lawsuit]. I thought that if you told the truth, you would win. What I learned was that the truth doesn't matter. It doesn't come down to who was right and who was wrong, but who is stronger.

When it was finally over, I didn't get the ending I thought I would. The courts wouldn't even hear the case, but I still feel a sense of vindication. Because I fought so long and so hard, people believed me. And, of course, now all studios have day care centers and everyone has a better understanding of why infants need to be with their mothers during their formative years.

It also opened my life and my work and pushed me back into the theater in a big way. Without it, I probably wouldn't have written *Shakespeare*. I didn't write it as therapy; I wrote it because I needed a job.

But somewhere along the way, healing was taking place. I try to be as emotionally honest as I can. The end result is that, when I've done it, I feel better and better toward my father. And I do forgive, although I don't think I could have forgiven without the play. But I don't think you can forget. I don't think you should . . . one can learn from these things.

If I hadn't written *Shakespeare* I wouldn't have been in *Shine* or written a second play [*The Mandrake Root*]. I made that happen—not some clever agent, but me. I'm proof that good things can spring from pain.

I did have a midlife crisis at forty-three and, after a few months, I got quite bored with it. I never believed all these people who said life got better as you got older. How could it possibly? Wrinkles? Ugh. But the year I turned fifty was actually one of the most satisfying of my life.

"I am not a has-been. I'm a will-be."

—LAUREN BACALL, actress

Great Quotes from Great Women

LINDA RONSTADT

© Robert Blakeman

130

After thirty years in the music business, Linda Ronstadt's career has been as remarkable for its versatility as its longevity. She has taken risks that few other artists would dare, traveling from rock to country to pop to Broadway to Mexican and Afro-Cuban music—and back again.

A veteran of the Los Angeles coffeehouse folk scene in the late 1960s, Ronstadt hit it big in 1975 with Heart Like a Wheel *and its chart-topping single* "You're No Good." *Even back then, she marched to a* Different Drum, *the title of her second album.*

In 1996, she again stretched herself as an artist, compiling an eclectic batch of songs skillfully arranged as lullabies for children, called Dedicated to the One I Love. *The project—her twenty-ninth album—grew out of the adoption of her own two children, now five and two.*

As always, Ronstadt was concerned with remaining true to the spirit of the material, but she was also concerned with staying close to her kids. So she managed both by setting up a studio in her San Francisco home.

* * *

Growing up in the rural West, I always felt different from other kids. We weren't like the people I saw in my *Dick and Jane* book. We didn't eat Wonder Bread, we ate tortillas. I never felt like I really fit in. But now I realize it was a blessing. Never identifying with mainstream American culture is what allowed me the freedom to explore different genres. I was fortunate that I didn't have to pin my career on one style, so the music always stayed fresh.

People ask me if, being in this business, I worried about job security. Well, one of the things you realize as you get older is that there really is no such thing as security anywhere . . . except in smaller, like-minded units of people. Fortunately, I have a nice family. I liked singing with them and the music held us together. The truth is that no one sounded as good with me as my dad, my brothers, my sister, and my cousins. I always wanted to be around family and I'm happy to get back to it whenever I can. When families are estranged, it's unspeakably sad. I always felt as if your family is there to protect you from your husband and your husband is there to protect you from your family.

> "So, life changes. And if you want to do what's authentic, you have to change, too."

Another thing I've learned is you have to pay attention to what's authentic. For me to do a song about youthful rebellion just doesn't ring true anymore. So, I figured out how to get out of that box. I did it with Gilbert and Sullivan, with Nelson Riddle standards, with jazz, gospel, and with the Mexican music that I felt was my birthright. I didn't have to perform some mediocre pop song when I knew that I had better stuff—real stuff—at home.

I remember hearing an old Gypsy woman in a club. She was singing the whole story of her life—all the men that had done her wrong, the babies, the disappointments. She wasn't up onstage like some twenty-year-old wannabe, but as a full-fledged sixty-year-old woman singing about all the riches of life, and I was blown away. That's what I want to be like.

So, life changes. And if you want to do what's authentic, you have to change, too. I don't like change, but I've learned, you just put your hands over your eyes and step off the edge.

The truth is that if you're in a place that is not you—a place that will drain your soul—it ultimately won't appeal to anyone else either. I'd rather fail with music that is really me than with something false. If you measure success by the applause or the money, you're already in trouble.

DIANE SAWYER

Not everyone could make the leap from Junior Miss Pageant winner to respected journalist, but Diane Sawyer has always believed all things are possible—providing you are willing to work hard enough.

"Besides," she says, "it taught me how to think on my feet."

It was a quality that would serve her well. In 1970, after a brief stint as a weathergirl and a part-time correspondent for the ABC affiliate in Louisville, Kentucky, Sawyer went to work for Richard Nixon in the White House press office. As the Watergate saga unfolded, she developed an even closer relationship with the embattled president, even moving to San Clemente to assist him in the writing of his memoirs. But once that task was completed, she was eager to return to her "former life"—this time, as a general assignment reporter for CBS News.

Such partisanship might have derailed other careers, but Sawyer restored her credibility with her balanced reporting and crisp writing. She was able to eventually win over her co-workers by her willingness to work the worst shifts.

She moved rapidly through the ranks—first, to CBS This Morning, *then to the most coveted job in her field: correspondent on* 60 Minutes, *before moving to ABC, where she is at the helm of the newsmagazine* Prime Time Live. *She lives in New York with husband/ director Mike Nichols.*

●　　●　　●

When I look back, I realize that it really is the cliché journey and not the destination that gives you joy. So I try to slow down, appreciate life more . . . and not let the little things defeat me.

When I look forward, I don't think we boomers will go gently into our senior years . . . that we will have to be dragged—kicking and screaming—all the way. As a generation, we've always assumed we are the center of all known vitality and we'll continue to feel that way well into our eighties. I can't believe we will settle for gray hair and a paunch. All that frenetic activity—all that flailing about at the gym—will pay off, and I applaud everyone who does it, because I certainly haven't.

What I don't understand is this assumption that aging means isolation. There's just so much to do in the world—so many people who need an ally, so many children who need hugging. I refuse to believe being elderly and being lonely go hand in hand.

Perhaps the reason that aging doesn't frighten me is that, over the years, I have done a number of stories on people who are graceful,

"We should be incubating something new—a second career, a more passionate hobby for the later

acute, and full of sparkle well into their nineties. They have sort of shown me the way. What they all had in common was this utter joy in their work. So right now—as we hit fifty—is when we should be incubating something new—a second career, a more passionate hobby for the later years—just to make sure that we're stretching and growing and not just repeating ourselves. For me? I'd like to be the first geriatric winner of the U.S. Open [tennis].

Or, I might follow the advice of Beatrice Wood—a potter who [had] lived in the south of France, whom we once did a piece on. Her prescription for staying youthful? Lots of young men and chocolates.

135

years—just to make sure that we're stretching and growing and not just repeating ourselves."

DONNA SHALALA

FEBRUARY 14, 1941
SECRETARY, DEPARTMENT OF
HEALTH AND HUMAN SERVICES

136

courtesy of Department of Health and Human Services

As head of the Department of Health and Human Services, Donna Shalala is known for her administrative skill, fiscal shrewdness, and unmatched energy.

In her position—where she oversees 59,000 employees and a $354 billion budget—Shalala needs hefty doses of all three. Currently on her to-do list: making health care more affordable, children healthier, and generating more resources for basic science and technology research.

Exhausting? Indeed. But Shalala is no stranger to running complex bureaucracies. Before joining President Clinton's cabinet, she was president of the University of Wisconsin, where she was the first woman to head a Big 10 University. At Madison, she is credited with taking fund-raising to new heights, strengthening undergraduate education, and even beefing up the football program.

Such talent was nurtured at an early age during a "blissfully secure" childhood in Cleveland. Her Lebanese-American parents passed along an immigrant's zeal to succeed; her mother became a lawyer by attending night school.

Wherever Shalala has been, say admirers and detractors alike, she has awed people with her dizzying pace. One former colleague called her ability to move through a cocktail party "like a fire crossing an oil slick."

She is single and lives in Washington.

＊　＊　＊

What I didn't realize when I was younger was the importance of fundamentals—to think clearly, to listen well, to speak articulately, to act decisively. A lot of emphasis is often placed on style, but I wasn't aware of just how valuable these basics would be later in life.

Also, I am reaping the benefits now of keeping myself in good physical shape. I play a lot of tennis and golf, I eat right, I don't smoke and all of that is paying off for me now. At fifty, it's far more important to be well rested because you are hired for your judgment, not your stamina. If you aren't rested, you aren't going to be very effective.

Then, there is the importance of a broad range of interests. I go to the theater, get together with close friends and family. That's why so many careers flatten out at fifty—because these people never did anything except work and then they burn out. As you get older, you have to be more aware of pacing yourself.

137

"At fifty, it's far more important to be well rested because you are hired for your judgment, not your stamina."

Humor, quick wit, charm, the ability to talk about something besides your work . . . all will serve you far better over the long haul than spending more hours at the office.

Reaching out across the generations is another way to stay involved, too. You can never grow old when you're surrounded by young people. And you always have to create more challenges for yourself. I never think about age because there's so much to do. There are so many mountains to climb before I reach sixty.

SUZANNE SOMERS

OCTOBER 16, 1946
ACTRESS

Jeff Katz © 1996

139

It would be so easy to dismiss Suzanne Somers as a dumb blonde, to assume that she is just an extension of the character she played on Three's Company, *the sitcom that propelled her to fame during the 1970s.*

But how many bimbos oversee a plethora of businesses, from videos to exercise equipment (including the infamous Thighmaster)? Perform hundreds of club dates a year or have written three books? Only by succeeding in vastly different arenas has Somers been able to prove that her success was not a fluke.

After years of a hand-to-mouth existence, she landed her first movie role in 1973 as the unattainable dream girl driving the '57 Thunderbird in American Graffiti. *It earned her $137 and cinematic immortality.*

Shortly after, she won the part of ditzy Chrissy Snow, which she played for four seasons until she was fired over a contract dispute. "That was a turning point. After so many years of struggling, I had finally gotten my foot in the door of this business and I wasn't about to just slink away."

When she found herself unemployable in TV, she put together a nightclub act. She also went to work on her autobiography, Keeping Secrets, *chronicling her life as the child of an abusive alcoholic, which was a fixture on the* New York Times *best-seller list for twenty-one weeks. Subsequent literary efforts include* Wednesday's Children, *on adult survivors of abuse, and* Suzanne Somers' Eat Great, Lose Weight.

Having done her penance, she was back in TV in the 1990s, with a comedy series, Step by Step, *the story of a blended family. It is a topic she knows well; she is married to her manager, Alan Hamel, whom she first met in 1968. Between them, they have two sons, one daughter, and three grandchildren.*

140

·　·　·

First, you have to take care of your emotional self. Get to the bottom of past experiences that keep you from being all you can be. I call it getting out of your own way. If you understand this, you can find forgiveness and let the past go. It's impossible to find serenity until the blockages are out of the way.

This was a huge revelation to me. As a child living with an alcoholic father, I learned early on that my feelings didn't count. My teenage marriage was doomed to fail because I didn't feel I had the right to express my feelings. I married this young man because I was told to do so, not because it was the right choice for my life. So I

"Get to the bottom of past experiences

married at seventeen, had a baby at eighteen, and was divorced at nineteen. I felt like such a failure. Only therapy helped me understand that in talking about my problems and writing them down, I could understand them. I wasn't able to even think about taking care of the exterior of me until I took care of the interior.

I love being fifty. I now have a perspective that lets me float above most situations. Frankly, I am happier with my looks today than I was before. I look in the mirror and see the real me. Diet and exercise play a part, but it's more. As a generation, we all actively went about the journey of finding personal happiness and growth, both emotionally and spiritually. I see it in so many men and women my age. Our eyes tell the truth; you can see the peace.

I admit I had a midlife crisis when my son told me I was becoming a grandmother. I think we always go kicking into the next passage. We're never ready. Two weeks after the announcement I went to my acupuncturist and said, "Maybe you should stick a couple of needles in for my emotions." He said, "You know, this is a great time in your life. You are preparing to be an elder of the tribe, a teacher . . . which brings respect and value." That snapped me right out of my funk.

Respect is a benefit of age. When I was playing the role of Chrissy, I was not taken seriously. It's a relief to not have that define me anymore. Now, when I conduct a business meeting, people listen to me. After all, they should. I own the company. Nothing in my twenties can compare to this time in my life.

Many men my age reach midlife and experience crisis. Often they leave their wives and marry younger women. All I can say is that they are losing out on the best part. I find this to be the most sensual and confident time yet.

that keep you from being all you can be. I call it getting out of your own way."

MARLO THOMAS

NOVEMBER 21, 1943
ACTRESS AND PRODUCER

142

She captivated America and became a role model for girls and women as the independent, single Anne Marie in the TV hit That Girl.

At the time, the notion that a woman didn't need a husband, children, or a suburban split-level to be fulfilled was revolutionary. Her popularity cast the prime-time mold for all other independent women, from The Mary Tyler Moore Show *to* Murphy Brown.

This was not some role that she just slipped into. She took the idea to the network and produced it as well. She has always had a strong independent streak, as evidenced by her social activism, her midlife marriage (in 1980, to talk show host Phil Donahue), and by her choice of projects. Her résumé includes the much praised bestseller (and later TV special) Free to Be . . . You and Me—*which she*

© Patrick Demarchelier

*created—aimed at countering sexual and ethnic stereotyping—the-ater (*Six Degrees of Separation, Thieves*), and film. Her mantel is graced by four Emmys, a Golden Globe, and a Peabody Award.*

After That Girl *ended in 1971, she moved in a completely new direction. "The last thing I wanted to do was repeat myself," she said. "I'm intrigued by the choice that isn't the safest."*

* * *

What you learn as you grow older is that no one can take anything away from you. You are the only one who can stop you from being the person you want to be.

When you're younger, you tend to blame other people—parents, siblings, spouse—but as you as you age, you see that you are the one in charge. It's a wonderful feeling because it puts you firmly in control. Once you blame others—even if it's justified—it puts you in a helpless position. It doesn't get you any-where, you can't change anything, so it's rather pointless. But once you see it as just background, then you can move ahead. You can say, "Where do we go from here?" And that's a very powerful stance.

> "You also realize how much both success and failure have to teach you."

You also realize how much both success and failure have to teach you. In any life, we'll get a full dose of both and we shouldn't be intimidated by either. It is the sad and painful parts of life—like the death of my father—that have really enriched me. They offer more opportunities for growth than all the good parts. The positive experiences fool you into believing that everything will always be okay—and that just isn't going to happen. I never really expected my father [actor Danny Thomas] to die . . . somehow, he convinced me that he would live forever—and in some ways, his spirit does. But if you can just endure the tough times, they will enrich your life.

When you're going through a really tough time, you need to have good women friends. Boys pick their friends based on sports. It's all about who can catch a ball or swing a golf club the best. But girls, from the time we're young, choose our friends based on who we can bare our souls to.

NINA TOTENBERG

Nina Totenberg will forever be known as the reporter who broke the story that shook the nation. But long before the names of Clarence Thomas and Anita Hill came on the scene, Totenberg was respected as a tenacious reporter who could take complex subjects and make them accessible to listeners.

An award-winning legal affairs correspondent, Totenberg joined National Public Radio in 1975. Her reports air regularly on the critically acclaimed newsmagazines All Things Considered *and* Morning Edition. *She has also contributed analysis for NBC News and ABC's Nightline.*

145

But it was her reporting about University of Oklahoma law professor Hill's allegation of sexual harassment by then–Supreme Court nominee Thomas that raised Totenberg's profile. The NPR veteran's reports led the Senate Judiciary Committee to reopen Thomas's confirmation hearings, netting her a fistful of hon-

© Murray Bognovitz

ors, *including the prestigious Peabody Award and the Alfred I.*
Dupont Award from Columbia University.

It was quite a climb from the women's pages of Boston's now-
defunct Record American *in 1965 to the Supreme Court beat.*
Perhaps Totenberg was so driven by the Thomas-Hill story because
at one of her early jobs, she, too, had been a victim of sexual harass-
ment. "There was nothing I could have done then, legally," she says.
"Had I been older and wiser and tougher, I might have done some-
thing, but when you're in your twenties, you just don't think you
have any recourse."

• • •

I was very glad that the Anita Hill story happened to me at forty-
seven and not twenty-seven. Senator [Alan] Simpson was trashing
me and I knew I couldn't lose my temper. So, I just concentrated on
saying my piece and not screwing up. It was the kind of situation
where only experience will save you. I was nervous, but I knew that
I didn't make any mistakes—I checked my facts fifty ways till
Sunday. Others were trying to discredit me because by discrediting
me they were discrediting the story, but I knew it was accurate.

I could have broken the story the night before, but it was more
important that I got it right, which is another benefit of age.
[*Newsday* reporter Timothy Phelps came out with his story on the
same day.] Some colleagues thought I should have gone ahead, but
I'm not sorry I waited because it was difficult enough.

The hardest part was when I left the *Nightline* studio and Alan
Simpson followed me into the parking lot, just screaming at me.
He called me a blankety-blank and I called him a blankety-blank
right back.

Now, we both feel that we didn't act appropriately and we both probably would have handled it differently. But I held it together. When I got home, I did what any professional woman would do—I buried my head in my husband's shoulder and burst into tears.

Sometimes you just gotta cry, but you never, ever do it in public. So here's my advice: It is a fact that you cannot swallow and cry at the same time. So grab your water jug and just keep swallowing. I'd like to have another big story like that . . . I just hope it's not a sex story.

"Sometimes you just gotta cry, but you never, ever do it in public."

In 1976, Diane Von Furstenberg's little wrap dress catapulted her to the top of the rag trade, showering her with both fame (she landed on the cover of Newsweek *and the* Wall Street Journal) *and fortune.*

She had found success with one basic design—a simple, sexy, body-hugging jersey—which offered both flattery and versatility for less than $100. At the height of its popularity, the wrap dress flew out of stores at the rate of fifteen thousand a week.

A few years later, the market had peaked. In addition, rapid expansion meant licensing, which resulted in a loss of control, a mistake Von Furstenberg vows she will never make again.

Born in Belgium to middle-class Jewish parents, she met Prince Egon Von Furstenberg—whose Prussian title goes back to the twelfth century—while attending college in Switzerland. They married in 1969 and moved to New York.

Having shown a flair for fashion, she used her connections to arrange a meeting with Diana Vreeland, Vogue's legendary editor. The rest is fashion history. "Her timing was everything," said Peg Zwecker, fashion editor of the Chicago Daily News.

Her home life, though, wasn't faring nearly as well. She and the prince divorced and she later moved to Paris. By 1990, she was back in the United States, ready to reclaim her position as an arbiter of style—this time in publishing. She turned out a lavish coffee table book, Beds, *followed by* The Bath *and* The Table.

But fashion was still in her blood. Today, she runs a full-service design and marketing studio and designs exclusive apparel lines for Avon, the Home Shopping Network, and Saks Fifth Avenue.

         ⊛   •   ⊛

149

> "Be your own best friend and don't forget to wink at yourself every now and then."

I learned that life is an extraordinary adventure and very few things are forever. I built this huge empire, pulled back and thought I was through. Then, I decided I wanted to come back—except people didn't take me very seriously. They saw me as a has-been. It was like "Who is she? Just because she was successful fifteen years ago, what makes her think she can be successful today?"

I met such resistance that I decided to go directly to the consumer with TV shopping, which was a revolution. It was a huge success . . . I sold $1.3 million of merchandise in two hours. It told me that people were ready to take me seriously again; it also convinced me to eliminate as many middlemen as possible—which is a pretty good philosophy for life.

Now, I'm working on a new line called "Diane"—very good-quality silks and jersey, but very affordable—something no one can do better than me.

What I've learned is this: Never lose control of the quality, the image, your name, which is all you have. Too many women listen to others when they should listen to their own instincts . . . be your own best friend and don't forget to wink at yourself every now and then.

As for age, it's not that looks don't matter—they do, and I certainly want to be as attractive as anyone can be—but you have to ask yourself, "How old is the heart?"

As I approached my fiftieth, I must confess that I didn't always feel this way. I had the entire year to think about this birthday and I was quite annoyed by it. But recently I've moved on to focusing on the significance of it: What it means to live this long—and to have been so privileged. I can't say I won't go under the knife, but I absolutely love the idea of never doing it.

There are some nice discoveries along the way: that if you wait long enough, the caravan comes by again. That you can now be friends with your kids. You don't just love them, but, if you are lucky, you like them. I'm quite impressed that somehow I made that happen. It's as if I planted these seeds and now it's harvest time.

FAYE WATTLETON

Ever since Margaret Sanger opened America's first birth control clinic in 1916, family planning programs have been denounced by everyone from politicians to the pope.

In 1978, when Faye Wattleton became president of Planned Parenthood Federation of America, it was still a lightning rod for controversy.

151

Wattleton was at the helm of the organization for fourteen of its most volatile years—when conservatives and the religious right were undeterred in their mission to chip away at reproductive rights.

© Albert Watson

They came up against a formidable foe. "Here is a person who does not accept the idea that some wrongs are just too hard to change," said David Andrews, a former Planned Parenthood colleague.

She came to activism quite naturally. Descended from a long line of quietly *determined African-Americans (her great-grandmother threatened a field boss with an ax when he came to take her son), Wattleton regularly traveled the revival meeting circuit with her fundamentalist preacher mother, who never approved of either birth control or abortion. ("When I resigned, she said, 'Thank God, my prayers have been answered.'")*

After entering Ohio State University at sixteen, she graduated with a nursing degree in 1964. Two years later, as a student midwife at Harlem Hospital, she first witnessed the devastating effects of illegal abortions.

In the 1990s, stories of corrosive chemicals and crude instruments may sound like science fiction, which is precisely why Wattleton included them in her memoir, Life on the Line. *She wanted young women to have a glimpse of life before* Roe v. Wade.

After resigning in 1992, she went on the lecture circuit and now is channeling her energy into a new project: the Center for Gender Equality, a New York–based think tank for women's issues.

She lives in New York and has a twenty-one-year-old daughter, Felicia, who is a student at Harvard.

. . .

What do I know now that I didn't know when I was younger? Two things—and they're both related.

The first is the danger of complacency and how easy it is to take things for granted. When young women tell me they are not feminists, I say, "Do you mean to tell me you don't believe in working in the best interest of women?" That's what feminism is—making sure that women are not limited in our options by virtue of their gender.

"We must do more to help our daughters understand

FAYE WATTLETON

Young women are where they are today because someone before them was willing to break some crockery.

Being a feminist doesn't mean that you're anti-male, but it does mean that you have an obligation to see that women's fundamental rights are preserved. Change takes a long time and we really need to stay with it. We must do more to help our daughters understand their own power and sense of purpose and value.

The second is the danger of subtlety. I now believe that things have to get really bad before women take a stand . . . before they're willing to fight, to weather criticism, to stop playing it safe and again push the envelope.

The [reproductive rights] battle is a power struggle over whether a woman will control the most private aspects of her body. It's more difficult today because the strategy is to take away the rights in increments. It's about RU-486, [the "morning-after" pill] and late-term abortions. It's about taking away your rights a little bit at a time by restraining women's abilities to exercise them.

Why do you have to be vigilant against subtlety? Because it's like rust on the fender of your car. You don't know it's there until it breaks through—then it's too late.

153

their own power and sense of purpose and value."

CHRISTINE TODD WHITMAN

SEPTEMBER 26, 1946
GOVERNOR OF NEW JERSEY

courtesy of New Jersey Office of Public Communications

She seemed to come out of nowhere, knocking out a powerful incumbent to become governor of New Jersey in 1993. Three years later, Christine Todd Whitman was on Bob Dole's vice presidential shortlist.

The meteoric rise was attributed to her centrist brand of Republicanism, one that combines the head of a fiscal conservative with the heart of a social moderate. Adjectives like "gracious" and "caring" have only enhanced her stock, particularly to women and minorities—two constituencies traditionally left outside the Republicans' big tent. "Imagine a Talbots catalogue with a sense of humor," describes the New York Times. *Her success is proof, say her supporters, that even in the 1990s an ordinary citizen can still capture the highest office in the state.*

While it's true that Whitman is a citizen, she is hardly ordinary. Growing up in a life of privilege, she felt politics was as natural "Another thing that gets better with age is your instincts. Learn to trust your gut reaction." *as oxygen. Her father, a successful builder, was head of New Jersey's Republican party, her mother, a delegate to national conventions. As a toddler, Christine had been bounced on Dwight Eisenhower's knee, and she counted Julie and Tricia Nixon among her girlhood friends.*

After graduating from Wheaton College (Massachusetts) in 1968, she spent four years in Washington working in several political jobs. Marriage to John Whitman, a Wall Street financier, was followed by two children. In 1982, she successfully ran for county freeholder—the first and only elected office she ever won before the governorship.

155

It wasn't until 1990—when she lost a Senate bid to Bill Bradley by only two percentage points—that she became a hot commodity. It galvanized her to take on Govenor Jim Florio, riding a tide of voter anger over taxes right into the statehouse.

Her most valuable political asset is her Teflon exterior. When she acknowledged that she and her husband failed to pay Social Security taxes for their nanny, she was lauded for her honesty. She even managed to extricate herself from the hiring of Larry McCarthy, a media consultant responsible for the Willie Horton ads (the controversial ads featured a black convicted murderer who raped a white woman in 1987 while on furlough). In editorial cartoons, Whitman showed up as the Energizer bunny, leaving a trail of gaffes in her wake.

But it is precisely the fact that Whitman does keep going and going that makes her one of the nation's highest-profile women.

· · ·

For all the bad things about politicians, you also see the true public servants. What really keeps you going is when you get the response from "real people."

When I signed the forty-eight-hour bill on minimal hospital stay for new mothers, the response from women was overwhelming. When you get to cut a ribbon for a new homeowner—usually a single mom—and the kids tell you how great it is to have a kitchen table, that feeling is so wonderful that it makes it easy to cope with the obstructionists. If you can hang on to what it is you're really trying to accomplish, that lesson works well outside politics, as well.

The value of negotiation is one of the true benefits of age. If you work hard enough, you discover that there's almost always a way to work things out, to step back and take another run at it. It may not be as neat and clean as you would like, but because of the negotiations, you frequently end up with a better product than what you started with. You learn to accept that you can't get everything done the way you like.

Another thing that gets better with age is your instincts. Learn to trust your gut reaction. When I was first campaigning for governor, I decided that I wasn't going to cancel our family vacation. I got a lot of grief for it. [Political advisers] were all over me and said that it proved that I wouldn't make a good candidate, but voters understood it and appreciated it.

On the other hand, the times I've gotten into trouble are when I didn't listen to my gut reaction.

Most of all, you've got to take opportunities as they open up. You can't sit there and plot a career because there are just too many variables.

"I already find myself being less rigid about all the things that I have to be and have to do.."

—NORMA KAMALI, designer

New Woman magazine

PHOTO CREDITS

Wattleton Christine Todd Whitman Gloria
Allred Carol Bellamy Linda Bloodworth-
Thomason Barbara Boxer Sarah Brady Dixie
Carter Nell Carter Cher Hillary Rodham
Clinton Jane Curtin Faye Dunaway Sandy
Duncan Linda Ellerbee Nora Ephron Jane
Fonda Nancy Friday Annette Funicello Phyllis
George Ellen Goodman Sue Grafton Marion
Hammer Valerie Harper Lauren Hutton Erica
Jong Naomi Judd Elaine Kagan Donna Karan
Diane Keaton Suzy Kellett Kay Koplovitz Patti
LaBelle Ellen Levine Donna Lopiano Susan Love
Tammy Faye Bakker Messner Carol Moseley-
Braun Anne Murray K. T. Oslin Letty Cottin
Pogrebin Stefanie Powers Lynn Redgrave Linda
Ronstadt Diane Sawyer Donna Shalala Suzanne